COLLECTED POEMS

PATRICK KAVANAGH

Collected Poems

Born in Inniskeen
Wrote during a psychological slump in
Ireland. After many wars, Ireland had its
national independence, but had lost all its
visions — people disinheadened and Ireland
isolated. Basically he wrote about bare facts
of living in concern with his own personal
experience

The Norton Library

W·W·NORTON & COMPANY·INC·

NEW YORK

To my Brother
PETER KAVANAGH

CONTENTS

II: 'The Great Hunger' and other poems

III: from 'A Soul for Sale'

IV: *Later Poems including 'Come Dance with Kitty Stobling'*

I

2

3

I HAVE never been much considered by the English critics. I suppose I shouldn't say this. But for many years I have learned not to care, and I have also learned that the basis of literary criticism is usually the ephemeral. To postulate even semi-absolute standards is to silence many lively literary men.

I would not object if some critic said I wasn't a poet at all. Indeed, trying to think of oneself as a poet is a peculiar business. What does it feel like to be a poet?

I am always shy of calling myself a poet and I wonder much at those young men and sometimes those old men who boldly declare their poeticality. If you ask them what they are, they say: Poet.

There is, of course, a poetic movement which sees poetry materialistically. The writers of this school see no transcendent nature in the poet; they are practical chaps, excellent technicians. But somehow or other I have a belief in poetry as a mystical thing, and a dangerous thing.

A man (I am thinking of myself) innocently dabbles in words and rhymes and finds that it is his life. Versing activity leads him away from the paths of conventional unhappiness. For reasons that I have never been able to explain, the making of verses has changed the course of one man's destiny. I could have been as happily unhappy as the ordinary countryman in Ireland. I might have stayed at the same moral age all my life. Instead of that, poetry made me a sort of outcast. And I was abnormally normal.

I do not believe in sacrifice and yet it seems I was sacrificed. I must avoid getting too serious.

I belong to neither of the two kinds of poet commonly known. There is the young chap who goes to school and university, is told by lecturers of the value of poetry, and there is the other kind whom we somehow think inspired. Lisping in numbers like Dylan Thomas, Burns, etc.

Looking back, I see that the big tragedy for the poet is poverty. I had no money and no profession except that of small farmer. And I had the misfortune to live the worst years of my life through a period when there were no Arts Councils, Foundations, Fellowships for the benefit of young poets.

On many occasions I literally starved in Dublin. I often borrowed a 'shilling for the gas' when in fact I wanted the coin to buy a chop. During the war, in Dublin, I did a column of gossip for a newspaper at four guineas a week.

I suppose when I come to think of it, if I had a stronger character, I might have done well enough for myself. But there was some kink in me, put there by Verse.

In 1942 I wrote *The Great Hunger*. Shortly after it was published a couple of hefty lads came to my lonely shieling on Pembroke Road. One of them had a copy of the poem behind his back. He brought it to the front and he asked me, 'Did you write that?' He was a policeman. It may seem shocking to the devotee of liberalism if I say that the police were right. For a poet in his true detachment is impervious to policemen. There is something wrong with a work of art, some kinetic vulgarity in it when it is visible to policemen.

The Great Hunger is concerned with the woes of the poor. A true poet is selfish and implacable. A poet merely states the position and does not care whether his words change anything or not. *The Great Hunger* is tragedy and Tragedy is underdeveloped Comedy, not fully born. Had I stuck to the tragic thing in *The Great Hunger* I would have found many powerful friends.

But I lost my messianic compulsion. I sat on the bank of the Grand Canal in the summer of 1955 and let the water lap idly on the shores of my mind. My purpose in life was to have no purpose.

Besides *The Great Hunger* there are many poems in this collection which I dislike; but I was too indifferent, too lazy to eliminate, change or collect. For these and other reasons I must offer thanks to Mr Martin Green who made the collection.

London 1964

BIBLIOGRAPHICAL NOTE

IT WAS not possible nor necessarily desirable to publish the poems in this volume in strict chronology. Part I contains the whole of *Ploughman and Other Poems* (Macmillan, 1936), Part II is concluded by *The Great Hunger* (Cuala Press, 1942), and Part III includes all the poems in *A Soul for Sale* (Macmillan, 1947), with the exception of *The Great Hunger*, previously mentioned, which first appeared, as it does here, unabridged. Part IV contains most of *Come Dance with Kitty Stobling* (Longmans, Green, 1960), though a number of these poems were written considerably earlier; these are therefore to be found in Part II, where they belong. The latter part of the book falls into three main groups, the divisions here being mostly of mood or theme, though Part 3 of Later Poems includes those most recently published.

Many of the poems in this collection first appeared in journals and magazines too numerous to mention here, and the publishers would like to make due acknowledgement to these, as well as to the publishers of the four books mentioned above.

I

'Ploughman and Other Poems'

PLOUGHMAN

I TURN the lea-green down
Gaily now,
And paint the meadow brown
With my plough.

I dream with silvery gull
And brazen crow.
A thing that is beautiful
I may know.

Tranquillity walks with me
And no care.
O, the quiet ecstasy
Like a prayer.

I find a star-lovely art
In a dark sod.
Joy that is timeless! O heart
That knows God!

TO A BLACKBIRD

O PAGAN poet you
And I are one
In this—we lose our god
At set of sun.

And we are kindred when
The hill wind shakes
Sweet song like blossoms on
The calm green lakes.

We dream while Earth's sad children
Go slowly by
Pleading for our conversion
With the Most High.

MARY

HER name was poet's grief before
Mary, the saddest name
In all the litanies of love
And all the books of fame.

I think of poor John Clare's beloved
And know the blessed pain
When crusts of death are broken
And tears are blossomed rain.

And why should I lament the wind
Of chance that brought her here
To be an April offering
For sins my heart held dear.

And though her passing was for me
The death of something sweet,
Her name's in every prayer, her charm
In every face I meet.

I MAY REAP

I WHO have not sown,
I too
By God's grace may come to harvest
And proud,
As the bowed
Reapers
At the Assumption
Murmur thanksgiving.

THE GOAT OF SLIEVE DONARD

I SAW an old white goat on the slope of Slieve Donard,
Nibbling daintily at the herb leaves that grow in the crevasses,
And I thought of James Stephens—
He wrote of an old white goat within my remembering,
Seven years ago I read—
Now it comes back
Full of the dreaming black beautiful crags.
I shall drink of the white goat's milk,
The old white goat of Slieve Donard,
Slieve Donard where the herbs of wisdom grow,
The herbs of the Secret of Life that the old white goat has nibbled,
And I shall live longer than Methuselah,
Brother to no man.

ASCETIC *- self-denial*

*intellectual
integrity*

THAT in the end
I may find
Something not sold for a penny
In the slums of Mind.

*get away
from the
emotional
mind-frustration
in Ireland*

That I may break
With these hands
The bread of wisdom that grows
In the other lands.

For this, for this
Do I wear
The rags of hunger and climb
The unending stair.

THE INTANGIBLE

Rapt to starriness—not quite
I go through fields and fens of night,
The nameless, the void
Where ghostly poplars whisper to
A silent countryside.

Not black or blue,
Grey or red or tan
The skies I travel under.
A strange unquiet wonder.
Indian
Vision and Thunder.

Splendours of Greek,
Egypt's cloud-woven glory
Speak not more, speak
Speak no more
A thread-worn story.

BEECH TREE

I PLANTED in February
A bronze-leafed beech,
In the chill brown soil
I spread out its silken fibres.

Protected it from the goats
With wire netting
And fixed it firm against
The worrying wind.

Now it is safe, I said,
April must stir
My precious baby
To greenful loveliness.

It is August now, I have hoped
But I hope no more—
My beech tree will never hide sparrows
From hungry hawks.

SOFT EASE

THE holes in my coat of want
Were the praise of good clothing.
Her chill indifference vaunt
Whom I loved was the proving
Of earnest young loving.

Now my chair of comfort is set
And the air in my room is warm,
Good things on my table, and yet
Beyond reach of my arm
The potion of charm.

The hand of Soft Ease is hard—
It was never raised in Heaven,
The eyes of Soft Ease are starred
In wastes where no driven
Truths have striven.

A STAR

BEAUTY was that
Far vanished flame,
Call it a star
Wanting better name.

And gaze and gaze
Vaguely until
Nothing is left
Save a grey ghost-hill.

Here wait I
On the world's rim
Stretching out hands
To Seraphim.

DARK IRELAND

WE ARE a dark people,
Our eyes are ever turned
Inward
Watching the liar who twists
The hill-paths awry.

Oh false fondler with what
Was made lovely
In a Garden!

TO A CHILD

CHILD do not go
Into the dark places of soul,
For there the grey wolves whine,
The lean grey wolves.

I have been down
Among the unholy ones who tear
Beauty's white robe and clothe her
In rags of prayer.

Child there is light somewhere
Under a star,
Sometime it will be for you
A window that looks
Inward to God.

NOT yet half-drest
O tardy bride!
And the priest
And the bridegroom and the guests
Have been waiting a full hour.

The meadow choir
Is playing the wedding march
Two fields away,
And squirrels are already leaping in ecstasy
Among leaf-full branches.

DREAMER

'A FOOL you are,' she said,
'Weaving dreams of blue
Deceiving sky. Evening folds them all
And what are you?
Squanderers of centuries and hours
Hold only faded flowers.'

'And why should I,' I answered,
'Walk among the dead?
And you are dead a million years,
The wolves are fed.
A fool who eats the leavings of the Wise,
Who tells me that he dies?'

GOLD WATCH

ENGRAVED on the case
House and mountain
And a far mist
Rising from faery fountain.

On inner case
No. 2244
Elgin Nath. . . .
Sold by a guy in a New York store.

Dates of repairs
1914 M. Y., 1918 H. J.,
She has had her own cares.

Slender hands
Of blue steel,
And within the precious
Platinum balance wheel.

Delicate mechanism
Counting out in her counting-house
My pennies of time.

SHE walked with me yesterday
Guiding my plough
Straight from headland to headland. . . .
Lament with me now.

My furrow twists like falsehood
The field's length and breadth.
O straight is truth I cry out
But my cry is death—

She will not come again
My furrow to guide,
For I have sinned against Guidance
And my plough has lied.

She will not come again
Till my field is ploughed—
I have not gone humbly cheerful
With shoulders bowed.

WORSHIP

To YOUR high altar I once came
Proudly, even brazenly, and I said:—
Open your tabernacles I too am flame
Ablaze on the hills of Being. Let the dead
Chant the low prayer beneath a candled shrine,
O cut for me life's bread, for me pour wine!

PHOENIX

SCRAP iron—
A brown mountain at the Dublin docks:—
Twisted motor chassis
Engines that once possessed creative energy
Stoves, wheels,
Jumbled tumbled
A catalogue-maker's puzzle.

Minds sicken
In the sight of these served-their-purpose things. . . .
A dead culture.

Yet somewhere up the river
The Life One sings:—
A Leeds furnace
Is the phoenix
From whose death-wings on this scrap-heap
Will rise
Mechanic vigour.
We believe.
Now is the Faith-dawn.

AFTER MAY

MAY came, and every shabby phoenix flapped
A coloured rag in lieu of shining wings;
In school bad manners spat and went unslapped—
Schoolmistress Fancy dreamt of other things.
The lilac blossomed for a day or two
Gaily, and then grew weary of her fame.
Plough-horses out on grass could now pursue
The pleasures of the very mute and tame.

A light that might be mystic or a fraud
Played on far hills beyond all common sight,
And some men said that it was Adam's God
As Adam saw before the Apple-bite.
Sweet May is gone, and now must poets croon
The praises of rather stupid June.

THE CHASE

I FOLLOWED Wisdom
A night and a night
And a day and a day
Clay-knowing to spite.

I went quickly
As gulls over fallow,
As goats among crags,
As winds through a hollow.

Yet never I
Caught up with slow-footed
Wisdom who took
The lanes deepest rutted.

She left me with
My gangster ambition
In remorse—and remorse
Is the Devil's contrition.

FOUR BIRDS

Kestrel

IN a sky ballroom
The kestrel
A stately dancer.
He is a true artist—
His art is not divorced
From life
And death.

Owl

Night-winged
As a ghost
Or a gangster,
Mystical as a black priest
Reading the Devil's Mass.

Lark

Morning star
Announcing the birth
Of a love-child.

Corn-crake

A cry in the wilderness
Of meadow.

BLIND DOG

I FOLLOW the blind dog
Over the twisted trail,
Bled by the wild-rose thorns
Where he lashes his comet tail.

I follow the blind dog,
Crying to my star: O star
Of a passionate pagan's desire,
Lead me to the truths that are.

TINKER'S WIFE

I SAW her amid the dunghill debris
Looking for things
Such as an old pair of shoes or gaiters.
She was a young woman,
A tinker's wife.
Her face had streaks of care
Like wires across it,
But she was supple
As a young goat
On a windy hill.

She searched on the dunghill debris,
Tripping gingerly
Over tin canisters
And sharp-broken
Dinner plates.

APRIL

Now is the hour we rake out the ashes
Of the spirit-fires winter-kindled.
This old temple must fall,
We dare not leave it
Dark, unlovely, deserted.
Level! O level it down!
Here we are building a bright new town.

The old cranky spinster is dead
Who fed us cold flesh.
And in the green meadows
The maiden of Spring is with child
By the Holy Ghost.

TO A CHILD

O CHILD, will you now share with me
The laughter of wise innocence?
My seer is love's infirmity!
My seer is love's incompetence.

Child, remember this high dunce
Had laughter in his heart and eyes,
A million echoes distant thence,
Ere Dublin taught him to be wise.

Sour is he as spinster's mouth
At kissing-time or time of praise,
His well of gladness dry, the drouth
Of desert knowledge is his days.

O child of laughter, I will go
The meadow ways with you, and there
We'll find much brighter stars than know
Old Aldebaran or the Bear.

INNISKEEN ROAD: JULY EVENING

THE bicycles go by in twos and threes—
There's a dance in Billy Brennan's barn to-night,
And there's the half-talk code of mysteries
And the wink-and-elbow language of delight.
Half-past eight and there is not a spot
Upon a mile of road, no shadow thrown
That might turn out a man or woman, not
A footfall tapping secrecies of stone.

I have what every poet hates in spite
Of all the solemn talk of contemplation.
Oh, Alexander Selkirk knew the plight
Of being king and government and nation.
A road, a mile of kingdom, I am king
Of banks and stones and every blooming thing.

PIONEERS

THEY wandered through the dark places and they kept
The prideful passionate horse tight-reined that would have leapt
The fence dividing star from meaner dust,
To trample down the corn which yields all men a crust.

They hungered as they went the sharp-stoned road,
And only one small lamp above them glowed. . . .
I too have eaten of the holy bread,
A crust they spared for me who no name had.

A WIND

THERE'S a wind blowing
Cold through the corridors,
A ghost-wind,
The flapping of defeated wings.
A hell-fantasy
From meadows damned
To eternal April.

And listening, listening
To the wind
I hear
The throat-rattle of dying men,
From whose ears oozes
Foamy blood,
Throttled in a brothel.

I see brightly
In the wind vacancies
Saint Thomas Aquinas
And
Poetry blossoms
Excitingly
As the first flower of truth.

AT NOON

I WILL not burn these rags,
The cast-off clothing of my soul,
In the chill of dawn they covered
Its nude ugliness.

Now in the passionate noon
The no-good dames
Tattoo my flesh with the indelible
Ink of lust.

What are these dim rooms
And red ghost-lamps?
Tell me this city's name,
New York or Paris?

Heaven was somewhere about
A child ideal.
Ah! the disillusioned one cried,
You have come far.

MARCH

THE trees were in suspense,
Listening with an intense
Anxiety for the Word
That in the Beginning stirred
The dark-branched Tree
Of Humanity.

Subjectively the dogs
Hunted the muted bogs,
The horses suppressed their neighing,
No donkey-kind was braying,
The hare and rabbit under—
Stood the cause of wonder.

The blackbird of the yew
Alone broke the two
Minutes' silence
With a new poem's violence.
A tomboy scare that drove
Faint thoughts of active love.

MORNING

Do NOT awake the academic scholars,
Tradition's hairy god last night departed.
This morn the huge iconoclastic rollers
Blot out the roads where long the Spirit carted
The prayerful dream, the scientific load,
The cobwebbed preacher-stuff of Portobello.
To-day will find a new straw-bodied god
Much brighter than the other morbid fellow.

And when they wake—the scholars—they will be
Toothless, unvoiced and maybe half-way gone,
With nothing but a clouded memory
To lead them to the hieroglyphic stone
On which old Scholarship had proudly scratched
A list of doors that Truth had left unlatched.

II

'The Great Hunger' and Other Poems

Now leave the check-reins slack,
The seed is flying far to-day—
The seed like stars against the black
Eternity of April clay.

This seed is potent as the seed
Of knowledge in the Hebrew Book,
So drive your horses in the creed
Of God the Father as a stock.

Forget the men on Brady's hill.
Forget what Brady's boy may say.
For destiny will not fulfil
Unless you let the harrow play.

Forget the worm's opinion too
Of hooves and pointed harrow-pins,
For you are driving your horses through
The mist where Genesis begins.

Monaghan 1933

PLOUGH HORSES

THEIR glossy flanks and manes outshone
The flying splinters of the sun.

The tranquil rhythm of that team
Was as slow flowing meadow stream.

And I saw Phidias's chisel there—
An ocean stallion, mountain mare—

Seeing with eyes the Spirit unsealed
Plough-horses in a quiet field.

ON AN apple-ripe September morning
Through the mist-chill fields I went
With a pitch-fork on my shoulder
Less for use than for devilment.

The threshing mill was set-up, I knew,
In Cassidy's haggard last night,
And we owed them a day at the threshing
Since last year. O it was delight

To be paying bills of laughter
And chaffy gossip in kind
With work thrown in to ballast
The fantasy-soaring mind.

As I crossed the wooden bridge I wondered
As I looked into the drain
If ever a summer morning should find me
Shovelling up eels again.

And I thought of the wasps' nest in the bank
And how I got chased one day
Leaving the drag and the scraw-knife behind,
How I covered my face with hay.

The wet leaves of the cocksfoot
Polished my boots as I
Went round by the glistening bog-holes
Lost in unthinking joy.

I'll be carrying bags to-day, I mused,
The best job at the mill
With plenty of time to talk of our loves
As we wait for the bags to fill.

Maybe Mary might call round . . .
And then I came to the haggard gate,
And I knew as I entered that I had come
Through fields that were part of no earthly estate.

MY ROOM

10 by 12
And a low roof
If I stand by the side wall
My head feels the reproof.

Five holy pictures
Hang on the walls:
The Virgin and Child
St Anthony of Padua
Leo the XIII
St Patrick and the Little Flower.

My bed in the centre
So many things to me—
A dining table
A writing desk
And a slumber palace.

My room in a dusty attic
But its little window
Lets in the stars.

SHANCODUFF

MY BLACK hills have never seen the sun rising,
Eternally they look north towards Armagh.
Lot's wife would not be salt if she had been
Incurious as my black hills that are happy
When dawn whitens Glassdrummond chapel.

My hills hoard the bright shillings of March
While the sun searches in every pocket.
They are my Alps and I have climbed the Matterhorn
With a sheaf of hay for three perishing calves
In the field under the Big Forth of Rocksavage.

The sleety winds fondle the rushy beards of Shancoduff
While the cattle-drovers sheltering in the Featherna Bush
Look up and say: 'Who owns them hungry hills
That the water-hen and snipe must have forsaken?
A poet? Then by heavens he must be poor'
I hear and is my heart not badly shaken?

Monaghan 1934

PYGMALION—

I saw her in a field, a stone-proud woman
Hugging the monster passion's granite child,
Engirdled by the ditches of Roscommon,
Stone ditches round her waist like serpents coiled.
Her lips were frozen in the signature
Of Lust, her hair was set eternally,
No Grecian goddess, for her face was poor,
A twisted face, like Hardship's, to me.
And who she was I queried every man
From Balladreen to grassy Boyle
And all replied: a stone pygmalion
Once lipped to grey terrific smile
I said: At dawn to-morrow she will be
Clay-sensuous. But they only smiled at me.

PEACE

And sometimes I am sorry when the grass
Is growing over the stones in quiet hollows
And the cocksfoot leans across the rutted cart-pass
That I am not the voice of country fellows
Who now are standing by some headland talking
Of turnips and potatoes or young corn
Or turf banks stripped for victory.
Here Peace is still hawking
His coloured combs and scarves and beads of horn.

Upon a headland by a whiny hedge
A hare sits looking down a leaf-lapped furrow
There's an old plough upside-down on a weedy ridge
And someone is shouldering home a saddle-harrow.
Out of that childhood country what fools climb
To fight with tyrants Love and Life and Time?

Dublin 1943

31

THEN I saw the wild geese flying
In fair formation to their bases in Inchicore
And I knew that these wings would outwear the wings of war
And a man's simple thoughts outlive the day's loud lying.
Don't fear, don't fear, I said to my soul.
The Bedlam of Time is an empty bucket rattled,
'Tis you who will say in the end who best battles.
Only they who fly home to God have flown at all.

Dublin 1943

PURSUIT OF AN IDEAL

NOVEMBER is come and I wait for you still
O nimble-footed nymph who slipped me when
I sighted you among some silly men
And charged you with the power of my will.
Headlong I charged to make a passionate kill,
Too easy, far too easy, I cried then,
You were not worth one drop from off my pen.
O flower of the common light, the thrill
Of common things raised up to angelhood
Leaped in your flirt-wild legs, I followed you
Through April May and June into September,
And still you kept your lead till passion's food
Went stale within my satchel. Now I woo
The footprints that you make across November.

IN THE SAME MOOD

You will not always be far away and pure
As a word conceived in a poet's silver womb
You will not always be a metaphysical signature
To all the poems I write. In my bleak room
This very year by God's will you may be
A woman innocent in her first sin
Having cast off the immortality
Of the never-to-be-born. The violin
Is not more real than the music played upon it
They told me that, the priests—but I am tired
Of loving through the medium of a sonnet
I want by Man, not God, to be inspired.
This year O maiden of the dream-vague face
You'll come to me, a thing of Time and Space.

I

CLAY is the word and clay is the flesh
Where the potato-gatherers like mechanised scarecrows move
Along the side-fall of the hill—Maguire and his men.
If we watch them an hour is there anything we can prove
Of life as it is broken-backed over the Book
Of Death? Here crows gabble over worms and frogs
And the gulls like old newspapers are blown clear of the hedges, luckily.
Is there some light of imagination in these wet clods?
Or why do we stand here shivering?
                                        Which of these men
Loved the light and the queen
Too long virgin? Yesterday was summer. Who was it promised marriage to
    himself
Before apples were hung from the ceilings for Hallowe'en?
We will wait and watch the tragedy to the last curtain,
Till the last soul passively like a bag of wet clay
Rolls down the side of the hill, diverted by the angles
Where the plough missed or a spade stands, straitening the way.

A dog lying on a torn jacket under a heeled-up cart,
A horse nosing along the posied headland, trailing
A rusty plough. Three heads hanging between wide-apart
Legs. October playing a symphony on a slack wire paling.
Maguire watches the drills flattened out
And the flints that lit a candle for him on a June altar
Flameless. The drills slipped by and the days slipped by
And he trembled his head away and ran free from the world's halter,
And thought himself wiser than any man in the townland
When he laughed over pints of porter
Of how he came free from every net spread
In the gaps of experience. He shook a knowing head
And pretended to his soul
That children are tedious in hurrying fields of April
Where men are spanging across wide furrows.
Lost in the passion that never needs a wife—

The pricks that pricked were the pointed pins of harrows.
Children scream so loud that the crows could bring
The seed of an acre away with crow-rude jeers.
Patrick Maguire, he called his dog and he flung a stone in the air
And hallooed the birds away that were the birds of the years.

Turn over the weedy clods and tease out the tangled skeins.
What is he looking for there?
He thinks it is a potato, but we know better
Than his mud-gloved fingers probe in this insensitive hair.

'Move forward the basket and balance it steady
In this hollow. Pull down the shafts of that cart, Joe,
And straddle the horse,' Maguire calls.
'The wind's over Brannagan's, now that means rain.
Graip up some withered stalks and see that no potato falls
Over the tail-board going down the ruckety pass—
And *that's* a job we'll have to do in December,
Gravel it and build a kerb on the bog-side. Is that Cassidy's ass
Out in my clover? Curse o' God—
Where is that dog?
Never where he's wanted.' Maguire grunts and spits
Through a clay-wattled moustache and stares about him from the height.
His dream changes again like the cloud-swung wind
And he is not so sure now if his mother was right
When she praised the man who made a field his bride.

Watch him, watch him, that man on a hill whose spirit
Is a wet sack flapping about the knees of time.
He lives that his little fields may stay fertile when his own body
Is spread in the bottom of a ditch under two coulters crossed in Christ's
     Name.

He was suspicious in his youth as a rat near strange bread,
When girls laughed; when they screamed he knew that meant
The cry of fillies in season. He could not walk
The easy road to destiny. He dreamt
The innocence of young brambles to hooked treachery.
O the grip, O the grip of irregular fields! No man escapes.
It could not be that back of the hills love was free

And ditches straight.
No monster hand lifted up children and put down apes
As here.
                                  'O God if I had been wiser!'
That was his sigh like the brown breeze in the thistles.
He looks towards his house and haggard. 'O God if I had been wiser!'
But now a crumpled leaf from the whitethorn bushes
Dart like a frightened robin, and the fence
Shows the green of after-grass through a little window,
And he knows that his own heart is calling his mother a liar
God's truth is life—even the grotesque shapes of its foulest fire.

The horse lifts its head and cranes
Through the whins and stones
To lip late passion in the crawling clover.
In the gap there's a bush weighted with boulders like morality,
The fools of life bleed if they climb over.

The wind leans from Brady's, and the coltsfoot leaves are holed with rust,
Rain fills the cart-tracks and the sole-plate grooves;
A yellow sun reflects in Donaghmoyne
The poignant light in puddles shaped by hooves.

Come with me, Imagination, into this iron house
And we will watch from the doorway the years run back,
And we will know what a peasant's left hand wrote on the page.
Be easy, October. No cackle hen, horse neigh, tree sough, duck quack.

II

Maguire was faithful to death:
He stayed with his mother till she died
At the age of ninety-one.
She stayed too long,
Wife and mother in one.
When she died
The knuckle-bones were cutting the skin of her son's backside
And he was sixty-five.

O he loved his mother
Above all others.
O he loved his ploughs
And he loved his cows
And his happiest dream
Was to clean his arse
With perennial grass
On the bank of some summer stream;
To smoke his pipe
In a sheltered gripe
In the middle of July—
His face in a mist
And two stones in his fist
And an impotent worm on his thigh.

But his passion became a plague
For he grew feeble bringing the vague
Women of his mind to lust nearness,
Once a week at least flesh must make an appearance.

So Maguire got tired
Of the no-target gun fired
And returned to his headland of carrots and cabbage
To the fields once again
Where eunuchs can be men
And life is more lousy than savage.

III

Poor Paddy Maguire, a fourteen-hour day
He worked for years. It was he that lit the fire
And boiled the kettle and gave the cows their hay.
His mother tall hard as a Protestant spire
Came down the stairs barefoot at the kettle-call
And talked to her son sharply: 'Did you let
The hens out, you?' She had a venomous drawl
And a wizened face like moth-eaten leatherette.
Two black cats peeped between the banisters
And gloated over the bacon-fizzling pan.

Outside the window showed tin canisters.
The snipe of Dawn fell like a whirring stone
And Patrick on a headland stood alone.

The pull is on the traces, it is March
And a cold black wind is blowing from Dundalk.
The twisting sod rolls over on her back—
The virgin screams before the irresistible sock.
No worry on Maguire's mind this day
Except that he forgot to bring his matches.
'Hop back there Polly, hoy back, woa, wae,'
From every second hill a neighbour watches
With all the sharpened interest of rivalry.
Yet sometimes when the sun comes through a gap
These men know God the Father in a tree:
The Holy Spirit is the rising sap,
And Christ will be the green leaves that will come
At Easter from the sealed and guarded tomb.

Primroses and the unearthly start of ferns
Among the blackthorn shadows in the ditch,
A dead sparrow and an old waistcoat. Maguire learns
As the horses turn slowly round the which is which
Of love and fear and things half born to mind.
He stands between the plough-handles and he sees
At the end of a long furrow his name signed
Among the poets, prostitute's. With all miseries
He is one. Here with the unfortunate
Who for half-moments of paradise
Pay out good days and wait and wait
For sunlight-woven cloaks. O to be wise
As Respectability that knows the price of all things
And marks God's truth in pounds and pence and farthings.

IV

April, and no one able to calculate
How far is it to harvest. They put down
The seeds blindly with sensuous groping fingers,

And sensual sleep dreams subtly underground.
To-morrow is Wednesday—who cares?
'Remember Eileen Farrelly? I was thinking
A man might do a damned sight worse . . .' That voice is blown
Through a hole in a garden wall—
And who was Eileen now cannot be known.

The cattle are out on grass,
The corn is coming up evenly.
The farm folk are hurrying to catch Mass:
Christ will meet them at the end of the world, the slow and speedier.
But the fields say: only Time can bless.

Maguire knelt beside a pillar where he could spit
Without being seen. He turned an old prayer round:
'Jesus, Mary and Joseph pray for us
Now and at the Hour.' Heaven dazzled death.
'Wonder should I cross-plough that turnip-ground.'
The tension broke. The congregation lifted its head
As one man and coughed in unison.
Five hundred hearts were hungry for life—
Who lives in Christ shall never die the death.
And the candle-lit Altar and the flowers
And the pregnant Tabernacle lifted a moment to Prophecy
Out of the clayey hours.
Maguire sprinkled his face with holy water
As the congregation stood up for the Last Gospel.
He rubbed the dust off his knees with his palm, and then
Coughed the prayer phlegm up from his throat and sighed: Amen.

Once one day in June when he was walking
Among his cattle in the Yellow Meadow
He met a girl carrying a basket—
And he was then a young and heated fellow.
Too earnest, too earnest! He rushed beyond the thing
To the unreal. And he saw Sin
Written in letters larger than John Bunyan dreamt of.
For the strangled impulse there is no redemption. *crucial line*

39

And that girl was gone and he was counting
The dangers in the fields where love ranted
He was helpless. He saw his cattle
And stroked their flanks in lieu of wife to handle.
He would have changed the circle if he could,
The circle that was the grass track where he ran.
Twenty times a day he ran round the field
And still there was no winning-post where the runner is cheered home.
Desperately he broke the tune,
But however he tried always the same melody crept up from the background,
The dragging step of a ploughman going home through the guttery
Headlands under an April-watery moon.
Religion, the fields and the fear of the Lord
And Ignorance giving him the coward's blow,
He dare not rise to pluck the fantasies
From the fruited Tree of Life. He bowed his head
And saw a wet weed twined about his toe.

V

Evening at the cross-roads—
Heavy heads nodding out words as wise
As the rumination of cows after milking.
From the ragged road surface a boy picks up
A piece of gravel and stares at it—and then
He flings it across the elm tree on to the railway.
It means nothing,
Not a damn thing.
Somebody is coming over the metal railway bridge
And his hobnailed boots on the arches sound like a gong
Calling men awake. But the bridge is too narrow—
The men lift their heads a moment. That was only John,
So they dream on.

Night in the elms, night in the grass.
O we are too tired to go home yet. Two cyclists pass
Talking loudly of Kitty and Molly—
Horses or women? wisdom or folly?

A door closes on an evicted dog
Where prayers begin in Barney Meegan's kitchen;
Rosie curses the cat between her devotions;
The daughter prays that she may have three wishes—
Health and wealth and love—
From the fairy who is faith or hope or compounds of.

At the cross-roads the crowd had thinned out:
Last words are uttered. There is no to-morrow;
No future but only time stretched for the mowing of the hay
Or putting an axle in the turf-barrow.

Patrick Maguire went home and made cocoa
And broke a chunk off the loaf of wheaten bread;
His mother called down to him to look again
And make sure that the hen-house was locked. His sister grunted in bed.
The sound of a sow taking up a new position.
Pat opened his trousers wide over the ashes
And dreamt himself to lewd sleepiness.
The clock ticked on. Time passes.

VI

Health and wealth and love he too dreamed of in May
As he sat on the railway slope and watched the children of the place
Picking up a primrose here and a daisy there—
They were picking up life's truth singly. But he dreamt of the Absolute
        envased bouquet—
All or nothing. And it was nothing. For God is not all
In one place, complete
Till Hope comes in and takes it on his shoulder—
O Christ, that is what you have done for us:
In a crumb of bread the whole mystery is.

He read the symbol too sharply and turned
From the five simple doors of sense
To the door whose combination lock has puzzled
Philosopher and priest and common dunce.

Men build their heavens as they build their circles
Of friends. God is in the bits and pieces of Everyday—
A kiss here and a laugh again, and sometimes tears,
A pearl necklace round the neck of poverty.

He sat on the railway slope and watched the evening,
Too beautifully perfect to use,
And his three wishes were three stones too sharp to sit on,
Too hard to carve. Three frozen idols of a speechless muse.

VII

'Now go to Mass and pray and confess your sins
And you'll have all the luck,' his mother said.
He listened to the lie that is a woman's screen
Around a conscience when soft thighs are spread.
And all the while she was setting up the lie
She trusted in Nature that never deceives.
But her son took it as literal truth.
Religion's walls expand to the push of nature. Morality yields
To sense—but not in little tillage fields.

Life went on like that. One summer morning
Again through a hay-field on her way to the shop—
The grass was wet and over-leaned the path—
And Agnes held her skirts sensationally up,
And not because the grass was wet either.
A man was watching her, Patrick Maguire.
She was in love with passion and its weakness
And the wet grass could never cool the fire
That radiated from her unwanted womb
In that country, in that metaphysical land
Where flesh was a thought more spiritual than music
Among the stars—out of reach of the peasant's hand.

Ah, but the priest was one of the people too—
A farmer's son—and surely he knew
The needs of a brother and sister.
Religion could not be a counter-irritant like a blister,

But the certain standard measured and known
By which man might re-make his soul though all walls were down
And all earth's pedestalled gods thrown.

VIII

Sitting on a wooden gate,
Sitting on a wooden gate,
Sitting on a wooden gate
He didn't care a damn.
Said whatever came into his head,
Said whatever came into his head,
Said whatever came into his head
And inconsequently sang.
While his world withered away,
He had a cigarette to smoke and a pound to spend
On drink the next Saturday.
His cattle were fat
And his horses all that
Midsummer grass could make them.

The young women ran wild
And dreamed of a child
Joy dreams though the fathers might forsake them
But no one would take them,
No one would take them;
No man could ever see
That their skirts had loosed buttons,
O the men were as blind as could be.
And Patrick Maguire
From his purgatory fire
Called the gods of the Christian to prove
That this twisted skein
Was the necessary pain
And not the rope that was strangling true love.

But sitting on a wooden gate
Sometime in July
When he was thirty-four or five

He gloried in the lie:
He made it read the way it should,
He made life read the evil good
While he cursed the ascetic brotherhood
Without knowing why.
Sitting on a wooden gate
All, all alone
He sang and laughed
Like a man quite daft,
Or like a man on a channel raft
He fantasied forth his groan.
Sitting on a wooden gate,
Sitting on a wooden gate,
Sitting on a wooden gate
He rode in day-dream cars.
He locked his body with his knees
When the gate swung too much in the breeze.
But while he caught high ecstasies
Life slipped between the bars.

IX

He gave himself another year,
Something was bound to happen before then—
The circle would break down
And he would curve the new one to his own will.
A new rhythm is a new life
And in it marriage is hung and money.
He would be a new man walking through unbroken meadows
Of dawn in the year of One.

The poor peasant talking to himself in a stable door—
An ignorant peasant deep in dung.
What can the passers-by think otherwise?
Where is his silver bowl of knowledge hung?
Why should men be asked to believe in a soul
That is only the mark of a hoof in guttery gaps?
A man is what is written on the label.
And the passing world stares but no one stops

To look closer. So back to the growing crops
And the ridges he never loved.
Nobody will ever know how much tortured poetry he pulled weeds on the
    ridge wrote
Before they withered in the July sun,
Nobody will ever read the wild, sprawling, scrawling mad woman's
    signature,
The hysteria and the boredom of the enclosed nun of his thought.
Like the afterbirth of a cow stretched on a branch in the wind
Life dried in the veins of these women and men:
The grey and grief and unlove,
The bones in the backs of their hands,
And the chapel pressing its low ceiling over them.

Sometimes they did laugh and see the sunlight,
A narrow slice of divine instruction.
Going along the river at the bend of Sunday
The trout played in the pools encouragement
To jump in love though death bait the hook.
And there would be girls sitting on the grass banks of lanes.
Stretch-legged and lingering staring—
A man might take one of them if he had the courage.
But 'No' was in every sentence of their story
Except when the public-house came in and shouted its piece.

The yellow buttercups and the bluebells among the whin bushes
On rocks in the middle of ploughing
Was a bright spoke in the wheel
Of the peasant's mill.
The goldfinches on the railway paling were worth looking at—
A man might imagine then
Himself in Brazil and these birds the birds of paradise
And the Amazon and the romance traced on the school map lived again.

Talk in evening corners and under trees
Was like an old book found in a king's tomb.
The children gathered round like students and listened
And some of the saga defied the draught in the open tomb
And was not blown.

45

X

Their intellectual life consisted in reading
Reynolds News or the *Sunday Dispatch*,
With sometimes an old almanac brought down from the ceiling
Or a school reader brown with the droppings of thatch.
The sporting results or the headlines or war
Was a humbug profound as the highbrow's Arcana.
Pat tried to be wise to the abstraction of all that
But its secret dribbled down his waistcoat like a drink from a strainer.
He wagered a bob each way on the Derby,
He got a straight tip from a man in a shop—
A double from the Guineas it was and thought himself
A master mathematician when one of them came up
And he could explain how much he'd have drawn
On the double if the second leg had followed the first.
He was betting on form and breeding, he claimed,
And the man that did that could never be burst.
After that they went on to the war, and the generals
On both sides were shown to be stupid as hell.
If he'd taken *that* road, they remarked of a Marshal,
He'd have . . . O they know their geography well.
This was their university. Maguire was an undergraduate
Who dreamed from his lowly position of rising
To a professorship like Larry McKenna or Duffy
Or the pig-gelder Nallon whose knowledge was amazing.
'A treble, full multiple odds. . . . That's flat porter . . .
My turnips are destroyed with the blackguardly crows. . . .
Another one. . . . No, you're wrong about that thing I was telling you. . . .
Did you part with your filly, Jack? I heard that you sold her. . . .'
The students were all savants by the time of pub-close.

<small>a learnéd
person</small>

XI

A year passed and another hurried after it
And Patrick Maguire was still six months behind life—
His mother six months ahead of it;
His sister straddle-legged across it:—
One leg in hell and the other in heaven

And between the purgatory of middle-aged virginity—
She prayed for release to heaven or hell.
His mother's voice grew thinner like a rust-worn knife
But it cut venomously as it thinned,
It cut him up the middle till he became more woman than man,
And it cut through to his mind before the end.

Another field whitened in the April air
And the harrows rattled over the seed.
He gathered the loose stones off the ridges carefully
And grumbled to his men to hurry. He looked like a man who could give
    advice
To foolish young fellows. He was forty-seven,
And there was depth in his jaw and his voice was the voice of a great cattle-
    dealer,
A man with whom the fair-green gods break even.
'I think I ploughed that lea the proper depth,
She ought to give a crop if any land gives. . . .
Drive slower with the foal-mare, Joe.'
Joe, a young man of imagined wives,
Smiles to himself and answered like a slave:
'You needn't fear or fret.
I'm taking her as easy, as easy as . . .
Easy there Fanny, easy, pet.'

They loaded the day-scoured implements on the cart
As the shadows of poplars crookened the furrows.
It was the evening, evening. Patrick was forgetting to be lonely
As he used to be in Aprils long ago.
It was the menopause, the misery-pause.

The schoolgirls passed his house laughing every morning
And sometimes they spoke to him familiarly—
He had an idea. Schoolgirls of thirteen
Would see no political intrigue in an old man's friendship.
Love
The heifer waiting to be nosed by the old bull.

The notion passed too—there was the danger of talk
And jails are narrower than the five-sod ridge

And colder than the black hills facing Armagh in February.
He sinned over the warm ashes again and his crime
The law's long arm could not serve with 'time'.

His face set like an old judge's pose:
Respectability and righteousness,
Stand for no nonsense.
The priest from the altar called Patrick Maguire's name
To hold the collecting-box in the chapel door
During all the Sundays of May.
His neighbours envied him his holy rise,
But he walked down from the church with affected indifference
And took the measure of heaven angle-wise.

He still could laugh and sing,
But not the wild laugh or the abandoned harmony now
That called the world to new silliness from the top of a wooden gate
When thirty-five could take the sparrow's bow.
Let us be kind, let us be kind and sympathetic:
Maybe life is not for joking or for finding happiness in—
This tiny light in Oriental Darkness
Looking out chance windows of poetry or prayer.

And the grief and defeat of men like these peasants
Is God's way—maybe—and we must not want too much
To see.
The twisted thread is stronger than the wind-swept fleece.
And in the end who shall rest in truth's high peace?
Or whose is the world now, even now?
O let us kneel where the blind ploughman kneels
And learn to live without despairing
In a mud-walled space—
Illiterate, unknown and unknowing.
Let us kneel where he kneels
And feel what he feels.

One day he saw a daisy and he thought it
Reminded him of his childhood—
He stopped his cart to look at it.
Was there a fairy hiding behind it?

He helped a poor woman whose cow
Had died on her;
He dragged home a drunken man on a winter's night;
And one rare moment he heard the young people playing on the railway stile
And he wished them happiness and whatever they most desired from life.

He saw the sunlight and begrudged no man
His share of what the miserly soil and soul
Gives in a season to a ploughman.
And he cried for his own loss one late night on the pillow
And yet thanked the God who had arranged these things.

Was he then a saint?
A Matt Talbot of Monaghan?

His sister Mary Anne spat poison at the children
Who sometimes came to the door selling raffle tickets
For holy funds.
'Get out, you little tramps!' she would scream
As she shook to the hens an armful of crumbs,
But Patrick often put his hand deep down
In his trouser-pocket and fingered out a penny
Or maybe a tobacco-stained caramel.
'You're soft,' said the sister; 'with other people's money
It's not a bit funny.'

The cards are shuffled and the deck
Laid flat for cutting—Tom Malone
Cut for trump. I think we'll make
This game, the last, a tanner one.
Hearts. Right. I see you're breaking
Your two-year-old. Play quick, Maguire,
The clock there says it half-past ten—
Kate, throw another sod on that fire.
One of the card-players laughs and spits
Into the flame across a shoulder.
Outside, a noise like a rat
Among the hen-roosts. The cock crows over
The frosted townland of the night.
Eleven o'clock and still the game

Goes on and the players seem to be
Drunk in an Orient opium den.
Midnight, one o'clock, two.
Somebody's leg has fallen asleep.
What about home? Maguire, are you
Using your double-tree this week?
Why? do you want it? Play the ace.
There's it, and that's the last card for me.
A wonderful night, we had. Duffy's place
Is very convenient. Is that a ghost or a tree?
And so they go home with dragging feet
And their voices rumble like laden carts.
And they are happy as the dead or sleeping . . .
I should have led that ace of hearts.

XII

The fields were bleached white,
The wooden tubs full of water
Were white in the winds
That blew through Brannagan's Gap on their way from Siberia;
The cows on the grassless heights
Followed the hay that had wings—
The February fodder that hung itself on the black branches
Of the hill-top hedge.
A man stood beside a potato-pit
And clapped his arms
And pranced on the crisp roots
And shouted to warm himself.
Then he buck-leaped about the potatoes
And scooped them into a basket.
He looked like a bucking suck-calf
Whose spine was being tickled.
Sometimes he stared across the bogs
And sometimes he straightened his back and vaguely whistled
A tune that weakened his spirit
And saddened his terrier dog's.
A neighbour passed with a spade on his shoulder
And Patrick Maguire bent like a bridge

Whistled—good morning under his oxter,
And the man the other side of the hedge
Champed his spade on the road at his toes
And talked an old sentimentality
While the wind blew under his clothes.

The mother sickened and stayed in bed all day,
Her head hardly dented the pillow, so light and thin it had worn,
But she still enquired after the household affairs.
She held the strings of her children's Punch and Judy, and when a mouth
    opened
It was her truth that the dolls would have spoken
If they hadn't been made of wood and tin—
'Did you open the barn door, Pat, to let the young calves in?'
The priest called to see her every Saturday
And she told him her troubles and fears:
'If Mary Anne was settled I'd die in peace—
I'm getting on in years.'
'You were a good woman,' said the priest,
'And your children will miss you when you're gone.
The likes of you this parish never knew,
I'm sure they'll not forget the work you've done.'
She reached five bony crooks under the tick—
'Five pounds for Masses—won't you say them quick.'
She died one morning in the beginning of May
And a shower of sparrow-notes was the litany for her dying.
The holy water was sprinkled on the bed-clothes
And her children stood around the bed and cried because it was too late for
    crying.
A mother dead! The tired sentiment:
'Mother, Mother' was a shallow pool
Where sorrow hardly could wash its feet. . . .
Mary Anne came away from the deathbed and boiled the calves their gruel.
O what was I doing when the procession passed?
Where was I looking?
Young women and men
And I might have joined them.
Who bent the coin of my destiny
That it stuck in the slot?
I remember a night we walked

Through the moon of Donaghmoyne,
Four of us seeking adventure,
It was midsummer forty years ago.
Now I know
The moment that gave the turn to my life.
O Christ! I am locked in a stable with pigs and cows for ever.

XIII

The world looks on
And talks of the peasant:
The peasant has no worries;
In his little lyrical fields
He ploughs and sows;
He eats fresh food,
He loves fresh women,
He is his own master
As it was in the Beginning
The simpleness of peasant life.
The birds that sing for him are eternal choirs,
Everywhere he walks there are flowers.
His heart is pure,
His mind is clear,
He can talk to God as Moses and Isaiah talked—
The peasant who is only one remove from the beasts he drives.
The travellers stop their cars to gape over the green bank into his fields:—

There is the source from which all cultures rise,
And all religions,
There is the pool in which the poet dips
And the musician.
Without the peasant base civilisation must die,
Unless the clay is in the mouth the singer's singing is useless.
The travellers touch the roots of the grass and feel renewed
When they grasp the steering wheels again.
The peasant is the unspoiled child of Prophecy,
The peasant is all virtues—let us salute him without irony
The peasant ploughman who is half a vegetable—
Who can react to sun and rain and sometimes even

Regret that the Maker of Light had not touched him more intensely.
Brought him up from the sub-soil to an existence
Of conscious joy. He was not born blind.
He is not always blind: sometimes the cataract yields
To sudden stone-falling or the desire to breed.

The girls pass along the roads
And he can remember what man is,
But there is nothing he can do.
Is there nothing he can do?
Is there no escape?
No escape, no escape.

The cows and horses breed,
And the potato-seed
Gives a bud and a root and rots
In the good mother's way with her sons;
The fledged bird is thrown
From the nest—on its own.
But the peasant in his little acres is tied
To a mother's womb by the wind-toughened navel-cord
Like a goat tethered to the stump of a tree—
He circles around and around wondering why it should be.
No crash,
No drama.
That was how his life happened.
No mad hooves galloping in the sky,
But the weak, washy way of true tragedy—
A sick horse nosing around the meadow for a clean place to die.

XIV

We may come out into the October reality, Imagination,
The sleety wind no longer slants to the black hill where Maguire
And his men are now collecting the scattered harness and baskets.
The dog sitting on a wisp of dry stalks
Watches them through the shadows.
'Back in, back in.' One talks to the horse as to a brother.
Maguire himself is patting a potato-pit against the weather—

An old man fondling a new-piled grave:
'Joe, I hope you didn't forget to hide the spade,
For there's rogues in the townland. Hide it flat in a furrow.
I think we ought to be finished by to-morrow.'
Their voices through the darkness sound like voices from a cave,
A dull thudding far away, futile, feeble, far away,
First cousins to the ghosts of the townland.

A light stands in a window. Mary Anne
Has the table set and the tea-pot waiting in the ashes.
She goes to the door and listens and then she calls
From the top of the haggard-wall:
'What's keeping you
And the cows to be milked and all the other work there's to do?'
'All right, all right,
We'll not stay here all night.'

Applause, applause,
The curtain falls.
Applause, applause
From the homing carts and the trees
And the bawling cows at the gates.
From the screeching water-hens
And the mill-race heavy with the Lammas floods curving over the weir.
A train at the station blowing off steam
And the hysterical laughter of the defeated everywhere.
Night, and the futile cards are shuffled again.
Maguire spreads his legs over the impotent cinders that wake no manhood
    now
And he hardly looks to see which card is trump.
His sister tightens her legs and her lips and frizzles up
Like the wick of an oil-less lamp.
The curtain falls—
Applause, applause.

Maguire is not afraid of death, the Church will light him a candle
To see his way through the vaults and he'll understand the
Quality of the clay that dribbles over his coffin.
He'll know the names of the roots that climb down to tickle his feet.
And he will feel no different than when he walked through Donaghmoyne.

If he stretches out a hand—a wet clod,
If he opens his nostrils—a dungy smell;
If he opens his eyes once in a million years—
Through a crack in the crust of the earth he may see a face nodding in
Or a woman's legs. Shut them again for that sight is sin.

one day one like the other

He will hardly remember that life happened to him—
Something was brighter a moment. Somebody sang in the distance.
A procession passed down a mesmerised street.
He remembers names like Easter and Christmas
By the colour his fields were.
Maybe he will be born again, a bird of an angel's conceit
To sing the gospel of life
To a music as flightily tangent
As a tune on an oboe.
And the serious look of the fields will have changed to the leer of a hobo
Swaggering celestially home to his three wishes granted.
Will that be? will that be?
Or is the earth right that laughs haw-haw
And does not believe
In an unearthly law.
The earth that says:
Patrick Maguire, the old peasant, can neither be damned nor glorified:
The graveyard in which he will lie will be just a deep-drilled potato-field
Where the seed gets no chance to come through
To the fun of the sun.
The tongue in his mouth is the root of a yew.
Silence, silence. The story is done.

He stands in the doorway of his house
A ragged sculpture of the wind,
October creaks the rotted mattress,
The bedposts fall. No hope. No lust.
The hungry fiend
Screams the apocalypse of clay
In every corner of this land.

any revelation
in a violent struggle
in which evil will
be destroyed

spiritual, intellectual and   1942
physical hunger of the Irish
countryman.

55

III

from 'A Soul for Sale'

MY SOUL was an old horse
Offered for sale in twenty fairs.
I offered him to the Church—the buyers
Were little men who feared his unusual airs.
One said: 'Let him remain unbid
In the wind and rain and hunger
Of sin and we will get him—
With the winkers thrown in—for nothing.'

Then the men of State looked at
What I'd brought for sale.
One minister, wondering if
Another horse-body would fit the tail
That he'd kept for sentiment—
The relic of his own soul—
Said, 'I will graze him in lieu of his labour.'
I lent him for a week or more
And he came back a hurdle of bones,
Starved, overworked, in despair.
I nursed him on the roadside grass
To shape him for another fair.

I lowered my price. I stood him where
The broken-winded, spavined stand
And crooked shopkeepers said that he
Might do a season on the land—
But not for high-paid work in towns.
He'd do a tinker, possibly.
I begged, 'O make some offer now,
A soul is a poor man's tragedy.
He'll draw your dungiest cart,' I said,
'Show you short cuts to Mass,
Teach weather lore, at night collect
Bad debts from poor men's grass.'
                    And they would not.

Where the
Tinkers quarrel I went down
With my horse, my soul.
I cried, 'Who will bid me half a crown?'
From their rowdy bargaining
Not one turned. 'Soul,' I prayed,
'I have hawked you through the world
Of Church and State and meanest trade.
But this evening, halter off,
Never again will it go on.
On the south side of ditches
There is grazing of the sun.
No more haggling with the world. . . .'

As I said these words he grew
Wings upon his back. Now I may ride him
Every land my imagination knew.

FATHER MAT

I

In a meadow
Beside the chapel three boys were playing football.
At the forge door an old man was leaning
Viewing a hunter-hoe. A man could hear
If he listened to the breeze the fall of wings—
How wistfully the sin-birds come home!

It was Confession Saturday, the first
Saturday in May; the May Devotions
Were spread like leaves to quieten
The excited armies of conscience.
The knife of penance fell so like a blade
Of grass that no one was afraid.

Father Mat came slowly walking, stopping to
Stare through gaps at ancient Ireland sweeping
In again with all its unbaptized beauty:
The calm evening,
The whitethorn blossoms,
The smell from ditches that were not Christian.
The dancer that dances in the hearts of men cried:
Look! I have shown this to you before—
The rags of living surprised
The joy in things you cannot forget.

His heavy hat was square upon his head,
Like a Christian Brother's;
His eyes were an old man's watery eyes,

Out of his flat nose grew spiky hairs.
He was a part of the place,
Natural as a round stone in a grass field;
He could walk through a cattle fair
And the people would only notice his odd spirit there.

His curate passed on a bicycle—
He had the haughty intellectual look
Of the man who never reads in brook or book;
A man designed
To wear a mitre,
To sit on committees—
For will grows strongest in the emptiest mind.

The old priest saw him pass
And, seeing, saw
Himself a mediaeval ghost.
Ahead of him went Power,
One who was not afraid when the sun opened a flower,
Who was never astonished
At a stick carried down a stream
Or at the undying difference in the corner of a field.

II

The Holy Ghost descends
At random like the muse
On wise man and fool,
And why should poet in the twilight choose?

Within the dim chapel was the grey
Mumble of prayer
To the Queen of May—
The Virgin Mary with the schoolgirl air.

Two guttering candles on a brass shrine
Raised upon the wall
Monsters of despair
To terrify deep into the soul.

Through the open door the hum of rosaries
Came out and blended with the homing bees.
                              The trees
Heard nothing stranger than the rain or the wind
Or the birds—
But deep in their roots they knew a seed had sinned.

In the graveyard a goat was nibbling at a yew,
The cobbler's chickens with anxious looks
Were straggling home through nettles, over graves.
A young girl down a hill was driving cows
To a corner at the gable-end of a roofless house.

Cows were milked earlier,
The supper hurried,
Hens shut in,
Horses unyoked,
And three men shaving before the same mirror.

III

The trip of iron tips on tile
Hesitated up the middle aisle,
Heads that were bowed glanced up to see
Who could this last arrival be.

Murmur of women's voices from the porch,
Memories of relations in the graveyard.
On the stem
Of memory imaginations blossom.

        In the dim
Corners in the side seats faces gather,
Lit up now and then by a guttering candle
And the ghost of day at the window.
A secret lover is saying
Three Hail Marys that she who knows
The ways of women will bring
Cathleen O'Hara (he names her) home to him.
Ironic fate! Cathleen herself is saying
Three Hail Marys to her who knows.
The ways of men to bring
Somebody else home to her—
'O may he love me.'
What is the Virgin Mary now to do?

From a confessional
The voice of Father Mat's absolving
Rises and falls like a briar in the breeze.
As the sins pour in the old priest is thinking
His fields of fresh grass, his horses, his cows,
His earth into the fires of Purgatory.
It cools his mind.
'They confess to the fields,' he mused,
'They confess to the fields and the air and the sky,'
And forgiveness was the soft grass of his meadow by the river;
His thoughts were walking through it now.

His human lips talked on:
'My son,
Only the poor in spirit shall wear the crown;
Those down
Can creep in the low door
On to Heaven's floor.'

The Tempter had another answer ready:
'Ah lad, upon the road of life
'Tis best to dance with Chance's wife
And let the rains that come in time
Erase the footprints of the crime.'

The dancer that dances in the hearts of men
Tempted him again:
'Look! I have shown you this before;
From this mountain-top I have tempted Christ
With what you see now
Of beauty—all that's music, poetry, art
In things you can touch every day.
I broke away
And rule all dominions that are rare;
I took with me all the answers to every prayer
That young men and girls pray for: love, happiness, riches—'
O Tempter! O Tempter!

As Father Mat walked home
Venus was in the western sky
And there were voices in the hedges:
'God the Gay is not the Wise.'

'Take your choice, take your choice,'
Called the breeze through the bridge's eye.
'The domestic Virgin and Her Child —
Or Venus with her ecstasy.'

Father Pat — dilemma whether to live + the lived of purgation and holiness or to give himself up to the sensuous world.

A POPLAR leaf was spiked upon a thorn
Above the hedge like a flag of surrender
That the year hung out. I was afraid to wonder
At capitulation in a field of corn.
The yellow posies in the headland grass
Paraded up and down in loud apparel;
If I could search their hearts I'd find a moral
For men and women—but I'd let them pass.
Hope guarantees the poor that they will be
Masters at haw-time when the robins are
Courageous as a crow or water-hen. O see
There someone on an ash tree's limb
Sawing a stick for a post or a drilling-bar!
I wish that I this moment were with him!

I should not have wished, should not have seen how white
The wings of thistle seeds are, and how gay
Amoral Autumn gives her soul away
And every maidenhead without a fight.
I turned to the stubble of the oats,
Knowing that clay could still seduce my heart
After five years of pavements raised to art.
O the devilry of the fields! petals that goats
Have plucked from rose bushes of vanity!
But here! a small blue flower creeping over
On a trailing stem across an inch-wide chasm.
Even here wild gods have set a net for sanity.
Where can I look and not become a lover
Terrified at each recurring spasm?

This time of the year mind worried
About the threshing of the corn and whether
The yellow streaks in the sunset were for fine weather.
The sides of the ricks were letting in; too hurried
We built them to beat the showers that were flying
All day. 'It's raining in Drummeril now,'
We'd speculate, half happy to think how

Flat on the ground a neighbour's stooks were lying.
Each evening combing the ricks like a lover's hair,
Gently combing the butt-ends to run the rain,
Then running to the gate to see if there
Was anybody travelling on the train.
The Man in the Moon has water on the brain!
I love one! but my ricks are more my care.

An old woman whispered from a bush: 'Stand in
The shadow of the ricks until she passes;
You cannot eat what grows upon Parnassus—
And she is going there as sure as sin.'
I saw her turn her head as she went down
The blackberry lane-way, and I knew
In my heart that only what we love is true—
And not what loves us, we should make our own.
I stayed in indecision by the gate,
As Christ in Gethsemane, to guess
Into the morrow and the day after,
And tried to keep from thinking on the fate
Of those whom beauty tickles into laughter
And leaves them on their backs in muddiness.

The air was drugged with Egypt. Could I go
Over the field to the City of the Kings
Where art, music, letters are the real things?
The stones of the street, the sheds, hedges cried, No.
Earth, earth! I dragged my feet off the ground.
Labourers, animals armed with farm tools,
Ringed me. The one open gap had larch poles
Across it now by memory secured and bound.
The flaggers in the swamp were the reserves
Waiting to lift their dim nostalgic arms
The moment I would move. The noise of carts
Softening into haggards wove new charms.
The simplest memory plays upon the nerves
Symphonies that break down what the will asserts.

O Life, forgive me for my sins! I can hear
In the elm by the potato-pits a thrush;

Rain is falling on the Burning Bush
Where God appeared. Why now do I fear
That clear in the sky where the Evening Star is born?
Why does the inconsequential gabble
Of an old man among the hills so trouble
My thoughts this September evening? Now I turn
Away from the ricks, the sheds, the cabbage garden,
The stones of the street, the thrush song in the tree,
The potato-pits, the flaggers in the swamp;
From the country heart that hardly learned to harden,
From the spotlight of an old-fashioned kitchen lamp
I go to follow her who winked at me.

BLUEBELLS FOR LOVE

THERE will be bluebells growing under the big trees
And you will be there and I will be there in May;
For some other reason we both will have to delay
The evening in Dunshaughlin—to please
Some imagined relation,
So both of us came to walk through that plantation.

We will be interested in the grass,
In an old bucket-hoop, in the ivy that weaves
Green incongruity among dead leaves,
We will put on surprise at carts that pass—
Only sometimes looking sideways at the bluebells in the plantation
And never frighten them with too wild an exclamation.

We will be wise, we will not let them guess
That we are watching them or they will pose
A mere façade like boys
Caught out in virtue's naturalness.
We will not impose on the bluebells in that plantation
Too much of our desire's adulation.

We will have other loves—or so they'll think;
The primroses or the ferns or the briars,
Or even the rusty paling wires,
Or the violets on the sunless sorrel bank.
Only as an aside the bluebells in the plantation
Will mean a thing to our dark contemplation.

We'll know love little by little, glance by glance.
Ah, the clay under these roots is so brown!
We'll steal from Heaven while God is in the town—
I caught an angel smiling in a chance
Look through the tree-trunks of the plantation
As you and I walked slowly to the station.

ADVENT

WE HAVE tested and tasted too much, lover—
Through a chink too wide there comes in no wonder.
But here in the Advent-darkened room
Where the dry black bread and the sugarless tea
Of penance will charm back the luxury
Of a child's soul, we'll return to Doom
The knowledge we stole but could not use.

And the newness that was in every stale thing
When we looked at it as children: the spirit-shocking
Wonder in a black slanting Ulster hill
Or the prophetic astonishment in the tedious talking
Of an old fool will awake for us and bring
You and me to the yard gate to watch the whins
And the bog-holes, cart-tracks, old stables where Time begins.

O after Christmas we'll have no need to go searching
For the difference that sets an old phrase burning—
We'll hear it in the whispered argument of a churning
Or in the streets where the village boys are lurching.
And we'll hear it among decent men too
Who barrow dung in gardens under trees,
Wherever life pours ordinary plenty.
Won't we be rich, my love and I, and please
God we shall not ask for reason's payment,
The why of heart-breaking strangeness in dreeping hedges
Nor analyse God's breath in common statement.
We have thrown into the dust-bin the clay-minted wages
Of pleasure, knowledge and the conscious hour—
And Christ comes with a January flower.

A CHRISTMAS CHILDHOOD

I

ONE side of the potato-pits was white with frost—
How wonderful that was, how wonderful!
And when we put our ears to the paling-post
The music that came out was magical.

The light between the ricks of hay and straw
Was a hole in Heaven's gable. An apple tree
With its December-glinting fruit we saw—
O you, Eve, were the world that tempted me

To eat the knowledge that grew in clay
And death the germ within it! Now and then
I can remember something of the gay
Garden that was childhood's. Again

The tracks of cattle to a drinking-place,
A green stone lying sideways in a ditch
Or any common sight the transfigured face
Of a beauty that the world did not touch.

II

My father played the melodeon
Outside at our gate;
There were stars in the morning east
And they danced to his music.

Across the wild bogs his melodeon called
To Lennons and Callans.
As I pulled on my trousers in a hurry
I knew some strange thing had happened.

Outside in the cow-house my mother
Made the music of milking;
The light of her stable-lamp was a star
And the frost of Bethlehem made it twinkle.

A water-hen screeched in the bog,
Mass-going feet
Crunched the wafer-ice on the pot-holes,
Somebody wistfully twisted the bellows wheel.

My child poet picked out the letters
On the grey stone,
In silver the wonder of a Christmas townland,
The winking glitter of a frosty dawn.

Cassiopeia was over
Cassidy's hanging hill,
I looked and three whin bushes rode across
The horizon—the Three Wise Kings.

An old man passing said:
'Can't he make it talk'—
The melodeon. I hid in the doorway
And tightened the belt of my box-pleated coat.

I nicked six nicks on the door-post
With my penknife's big blade—
There was a little one for cutting tobacco.
And I was six Christmases of age.

My father played the melodeon,
My mother milked the cows,
And I had a prayer like a white rose pinned
On the Virgin Mary's blouse.

MEMORY OF MY FATHER

EVERY old man I see
Reminds me of my father
When he had fallen in love with death
One time when sheaves were gathered.

That man I saw in Gardner Street
Stumble on the kerb was one,
He stared at me half-eyed,
I might have been his son.

And I remember the musician
Faltering over his fiddle
In Bayswater, London,
He too set me the riddle.

Every old man I see
In October-coloured weather
Seems to say to me:
'I was once your father.'

THE LONG GARDEN

IT WAS the garden of the golden apples,
A long garden between a railway and a road,
In the sow's rooting where the hen scratches
We dipped our fingers in the pockets of God.

In the thistly hedge old boots were flying sandals
By which we travelled through the childhood skies,
Old buckets rusty-holed with half-hung handles
Were drums to play when old men married wives.

The pole that lifted the clothes-line in the middle
Was the flag-pole on a prince's palace when
We looked at it though fingers crossed to riddle
In evening sunlight miracles for men.

It was the garden of the golden apples,
And when the Carrick train went by we knew
That we could never die till something happened
Like wishing for a fruit that never grew,

Or wanting to be up on Candle-Fort
Above the village with its shops and mill.
The racing cyclists' gasp-gapped reports
Hinted of pubs where life can drink his fill.

And when the sun went down into Drumcatton
And the New Moon by its little finger swung
From the telegraph wires, we knew how God had happened
And what the blackbird in the whitethorn sang.

It was the garden of the golden apples,
The half-way house where we had stopped a day
Before we took the west road to Drumcatton
Where the sun was always setting on the play.

PRIMROSE

Upon a bank I sat, a child made seer
Of one small primrose flowering in my mind.
Better than wealth it is, said I, to find
One small page of Truth's manuscript made clear.
I looked at Christ transfigured without fear—
The light was very beautiful and kind,
And where the Holy Ghost in flame had signed
I read it through the lenses of a tear.
And then my sight grew dim, I could not see
The primrose that had lighted me to Heaven,
And there was but the shadow of a tree
Ghostly among the stars. The years that pass
Like tired soldiers nevermore have given
Moments to see wonders in the grass.

ART McCOOEY

I RECOVER now the time I drove
Cart-loads of dung to an outlying farm—
My foreign possessions in Shancoduff—
With the enthusiasm of a man who sees life simply.

The steam rising from the load is still
Warm enough to thaw my frosty fingers.
In Donnybrook in Dublin ten years later
I see that empire now and the empire builder.

Sometimes meeting a neighbour
In country love-enchantment,
The old mare pulls over to the bank and leaves us
To fiddle folly where November dances.

We wove our disappointments and successes
To patterns of a town-bred logic:
'She might have been sick. . . . No, never before,
A mystery, Pat, and they all appear so modest.'

We exchanged our fool advices back and forth:
'It easily could be their cow was calving,
And sure the rain was desperate that night . . .'
Somewhere in the mists a light was laughing.

We played with the frilly edges of reality
While we puffed our cigarettes;
And sometimes Owney Martin's splitting yell
Would knife the dreamer that the land begets.

'I'll see you after Second Mass on Sunday.'
'Righ-o, right-o.' The mare moves on again.
A wheel rides over a heap of gravel
And the mare goes skew-ways like a blinded hen.

Down the lane-way of the popular banshees
By Paddy Bradley's; mud to the ankles;
A hare is grazing in Mat Rooney's meadow;
Maggie Byrne is prowling for dead branches.

Ten loads before tea-time. Was that the laughter
Of the evening bursting school?
The sun sinks low and large behind the hills of Cavan,
A stormy-looking sunset. 'Brave and cool.'

Wash out the cart with a bucket of water and a wangel
Of wheaten straw. Jupiter looks down.
Unlearnedly and unreasonably poetry is shaped
Awkwardly but alive in the unmeasured womb.

SPRAYING THE POTATOES

THE barrels of blue potato-spray
Stood on a headland of July
Beside an orchard wall where roses
Were young girls hanging from the sky.

The flocks of green potato-stalks
Were blossom spread for sudden flight,
The Kerr's Pinks in a frivelled blue,
The Arran Banners wearing white.

And over that potato-field
A lazy veil of woven sun.
Dandelions growing on headlands, showing
Their unloved hearts to everyone.

And I was there with the knapsack sprayer
On the barrel's edge poised. A wasp was floating
Dead on a sunken briar leaf
Over a copper-poisoned ocean.

The axle-roll of a rut-locked cart
Broke the burnt stick of noon in two.
An old man came through a cornfield
Remembering his youth and some Ruth he knew.

He turned my way. 'God further the work.'
He echoed an ancient farming prayer.
I thanked him. He eyed the potato-drills.
He said: 'You are bound to have good ones there.'

We talked and our talk was a theme of kings,
A theme for strings. He hunkered down
In the shade of the orchard wall. O roses
The old man dies in the young girl's frown.

And poet lost to potato-fields,
Remembering the lime and copper smell
Of the spraying barrels he is not lost
Or till blossomed stalks cannot weave a spell.

ETHICAL

You who have not sown
Will eat the bitter bread
And beg the sweetness of a stone
Flung at Saint Stephen's head.

You who have not sung
Will hear the clang of brass
When fairies beat on April's gong
With stems of greening grass.

And you who have not prayed
The blackbird's evening prayer
Will kneel all night dismayed
Upon a frozen stair.

SANCTITY

To be a poet and not know the trade,
To be a lover and repel all women;
Twin ironies by which great saints are made,
The agonising pincer-jaws of Heaven.

CANDIDA

FOR JOHN BETJEMAN'S DAUGHTER

CANDIDA is one to-day,
What is there that *one* can say?
One is where the race begins
Or the sum that counts our sins;
But the mark time makes to-morrow
Shapes the cross of joy or sorrow.

Candida is one to-day,
What is there for me to say?
On the day that she was one
There were apples in the sun
And the fields long wet with rain
Crumply in dry winds again.

Candida is one and I
Wish her lots and lots of joy.
She the nursling of September
Like a war she won't remember.
Candida is one to-day
And there's nothing more to say.

WAR AND PEACE

Do YOU hear that noise, Mother,
That comes over the sea?
Is that God the Father raging
In His Eternity?

That is only war, darling,
Drunk men returning
From the pubs of their pleasure,
They'll be sober by morning.

Do you hear that whisper, Mother,
That follows the sigh
From the house of Injustice?
What was that going by?

That was God raging, child,
Something to fright
More than the shouting
Of a whole drunken night.

STONY GREY SOIL

O STONY grey soil of Monaghan
The laugh from my love you thieved;
You took the gay child of my passion
And gave me your clod-conceived.

You clogged the feet of my boyhood
And I believed that my stumble
Had the poise and stride of Apollo
And his voice my thick-tongued mumble.

You told me the plough was immortal!
O green-life-conquering plough!
Your mandril strained, your coulter blunted
In the smooth lea-field of my brow.

You sang on steaming dunghills
A song of cowards' brood,
You perfumed my clothes with weasel itch,
You fed me on swinish food.

You flung a ditch on my vision
Of beauty, love and truth.
O stony grey soil of Monaghan
You burgled my bank of youth!

Lost the long hours of pleasure
All the women that love young men.
O can I still stroke the monster's back
Or write with unpoisoned pen

His name in these lonely verses
Or mention the dark fields where
The first gay flight of my lyric
Got caught in a peasant's prayer.

Mullahinsha, Drummeril, Black Shanco—
Wherever I turn I see
In the stony grey soil of Monaghan
Dead loves that were born for me.

It WOULD never be morning, always evening,
Golden sunset, golden age—
When Shakespeare, Marlowe and Jonson were writing
The future of England page by page
A nettle-wild grave was Ireland's stage.

It would never be spring, always autumn
After a harvest always lost,
When Drake was winning seas for England
We sailed in puddles of the past
Chasing the ghost of Brendan's mast.

The seeds among the dust were less than dust,
Dust we sought, decay,
The young sprout rising smothered in it,
Cursed for being in the way—
And the same is true to-day.

Culture is always something that was,
Something pedants can measure,
Skull of bard, thigh of chief,
Depth of dried-up river.
Shall we be thus for ever?
Shall we be thus for ever?

A WREATH FOR TOM MOORE'S STATUE

THE cowardice of Ireland is in his statue,
No poet's honoured when they wreathe this stone,
An old shopkeeper who has dealt in the marrow-bone
Of his neighbours looks at you.
Dim-eyed, degenerate, he is admiring his god,
The bank-manager who pays his monthly confession,
The tedious narrative of a mediocrity's passion,
The shallow, safe sins that never become a flood
To sweep themselves away. From under
His coat-lapels the vermin creep as Joyce
Noted in passing on his exile's way.
In the wreathing of this stone now I wonder
If there is not somehow the worship of the lice
That crawl upon the seven-deadened clay.

They put a wreath upon the dead
For the dead will wear the cap of any racket,
The corpse will not put his elbows through his jacket
Or contradict the words some liar has said.
The corpse can be fitted out to deceive—
Fake thoughts, fake love, fake ideal,
And rogues can sell its guaranteed appeal,
Guaranteed to work and never come alive.
The poet would not stay poetical
And his humility was far from being pliable,
Voluptuary to-morrow, to-day ascetical,
His morning gentleness was the evening's rage.
But here we give you death, the old reliable
Whose white blood cannot blot the respectable page.

Some clay the lice have stirred
Falls now for ever into hell's lousy hollows.
The terrible peace is that follows
The annihilation of the flesh-rotted word.
But hope! the poet comes again to build
A new city high above lust and logic,
The trucks of language overflow and magic
At every turn of the living road is spilled.

The sense is over-sense. No need more
To analyse, to controvert or turn
The laugh against the cynic's leer of power.
In his own city now he lives before
The clay earth was made, an Adam never born,
His light imprisoned in a dinner-hour.

IV

Later Poems including 'Come Dance with Kitty Stobling'

He SAID: The road you are going will lead you to Hate
For I went down that way yesterday and saw it away
In the hollow a mile distant and I turned back
Glad of my escape.
                But I said: I will persist,
For I know a man who went down the hill into the hollow
And entered the very city of Hate
And God visited him every day out of pity
Till in the end he became a most noble saint.

THE PADDIAD

IN THE corner of a Dublin pub
This party opens—blub-a-blub—
Paddy Whiskey, Rum and Gin
Paddy Three sheets in the wind;
Paddy of the Celtic Mist,
Paddy Connemara West,
Chestertonian Paddy Frog
Croaking nightly in the bog.
All the Paddies having fun
Since Yeats handed in his gun.
Every man completely blind
To the truth about his mind.

In their middle sits a fellow
Aged about sixty, bland and mellow;
Saintly silvery locks of hair,
Quiet-voiced as monk at prayer;
Every Paddy's eye is glazed
On this fellow. Mouths amazed
Drink in all his words of praise.
O comic muse descend to see
The devil Mediocrity,
For that is the devil sitting there,
Actually Lucifer.

He has written many Catholic novels,
None of which mention devils:
Daring men, beautiful women,
Nothing about muck or midden,
Wholesome atmosphere—Why must
So-called artists deal with lust?

About the devil's dark intentions
There are some serious misconceptions:
The devil is supposed to be
A nasty man entirely,
Horned and hoofed and fearful gory—
That's his own invented story.

The truth in fact is the reverse
He does not know a single curse;
His forte's praise for what is dead,
Pegasus's Munnings bred.
Far and near he screws his eyes
In search of what will never rise,
Souls that are fusty, safe and dim,
These are the geniuses of the land to him.

Most generous-tempered of the gods
He listens to the vilest odes,
Aye, and not just idle praise!
For these the devil highly pays.
And the crowds for culture cheer and cheer:
'A modern Medici is here,
Never more can it be said
That Irish poets are not fed'
The boys go wild and toast the Joker
The master of the mediocre.

'A great renaissance is under way'
You can hear the devil say
As into our pub comes a new arrival,
A man who looks the conventional devil:
This is Paddy Conscience, this
Is Stephen Dedalus,
This is Yeats who ranted to
Knave and fool before he knew
This is Sean O'Casey saying,
Fare thee well to Inishfallen.

He stands on the perimeter of the crowd
Half drunk to show that he's not proud
But willing given half a chance
To play the game with any dunce;
He wears a beaten bedraggled pose
To put the devil at his ease,
But Lucifer sees through the pose
Of drunken talk and dirty clothes;
The casual word that drops by chance
Denotes a dangerous arrogance,
Still sober and alive enough
To blast this world with a puff.

Every Paddy sitting there
Pops up like a startled hare,
Loud ignorings fill each face—
This behaviour's a disgrace,
A savage intruding on our Monday's
Colloquy on trochees, spondees,
And whether Paddy Mist or Frog
Is the greatest singer of the bog.
Hypodermics sourpiss loaded
Are squirted at our foolish poet.
The devil sips his glass of plain
And takes up his theme again:

'My suggestion is for a large bounty
For the best poet in each county.
How many poems, Mist, can you spare
For my new anthology of Clare?
Ten guineas per poem is fair,
But they must definitely be Clare;
Some lyrics in your recent volume
Were influenced by Roscommon'

Conscience: 'I'm a Clareman more than Mist'
Mist, 'But essentially a novelist'
Frog: 'Essentially a man of prose
As any whole-time verseman knows.
I think that Paddy Connemara West

92

Is worth twenty guineas at least'
'I agree, Frog
West is one of the great singers of the bog—
I'll give him twenty guineas, so—'

'Oh, oh, oh,'
Conscience is going mad,
Tearing, raving, using bad
Language in the bar
Where the bards of Ireland are.
Now peace again, they've chucked him out.
Paddy Frog leaves down his stout,
Clenches his chubby grocer's fist,
Says: 'I disagree with Mist
That Paddy Connemara West
Is inferior to Stephens at his best—
A Catholic and Gaelic poet,
His last group of poems show it'
Devil: 'Paddy Connemara gets my vote
As the expressor of the Catholic note,
His pious feeling for the body
And rejection of the shoddy
Mystical cloak that Conscience trails
Places him among the greatest of Gaels;
In my last radio talk I drew
Attention to this Froggish view.

We must bring out a Collected Edition
The money's a minor consideration—
What most we want to bring success
Is an end to petty bitterness,
No more slashing notices in the press
But something broadly generous
We want an openess of heart—
No Olympian critics saying: depart
From me ye cursed pack of fools,
Only poetasters form schools.
You remember Paddy Conscience
'Count me out at mummers' rantings'

Here news has just come in that Paddy
Conscience lost his latest body,
Dead in Paris—
The devil sighs—'Shocking news—
I much admired all his views.
A man of genius, generous, kind,
Not a destructive idea in his mind.
My dearest friend! Let's do him proud.
Our wives will make a green silk shroud
To weave him in. The Emerald Isle
Must bury him in tourist style.

A broadcast on his work might be
A reading of his poetry.
The Government will give a grant
To build a worthy monument,
I know the Minister involved,
The cost will readily be halved.
Before we part let's make a date
To meet tomorrow night at eight
To make the final funeral plans,
For this will be Ireland seen by France.
This is the window of our shop.
Paddy Mist might do an ap—
Preciation on the general
Culture of an Irish funeral'.

All the Paddies rise and hurry
Home to write the inside story
Of their friendship for the late
Genius who was surely great;
Recall his technical innovations,
His domestic life, his patience
With humblest aspirant
On the literary bent.

All his hunger was imagined,
Never was a false legend,
He could make whenever he chose
A fortune out of verse or prose.
Irish women spirituelle
Ran from race-tracks at his spell,
Left the beds of jockeys, actors—
These may be considered factors.

The group's dispersed. The devil stays,
Some discontent in his face.
Already he can see another
Conscience coming on to bother
Ireland with muck and anger,
Ready again to die of hunger,
Condemnatory and uncivil—
What a future for a devil!

JUNGLE

THROUGH the jungle of Pembroke Road
I have dragged myself in terror
Listening to the lions of Frustration roar,
The anguish of beasts that have had their dinner
And found there was something inside
Gnawing away unsatisfied.

As far as Ballsbridge I walked in wonder,
Down Clyde to Waterloo
Watching the natives pulling the jungle
Grass of Convention to cover the nude
Barbaric buttocks where tail-stumps showed
When reason lit up the road.

On Baggot Street Bridge they screeched,
Then dived out of my sight
Into the pools of blackest porter—
Till half-past ten of the jungle night
The bubbles came up with toxic smell
From Frustration's holy well.

THE DEFEATED

ALWAYS in pubs I meet them, the defeated,
With a long sweep of the face crying;
Ridiculous the idea that you have stated—
I lived ten years in that city, and you are lying
To say that houses with slate roofs exist,
With windows, wooden floors and rooms upstairs;
A dream, dear friend, there's no bed gives such rest
As a straw bed evenly spread. There are no powers
Greater than this most ancient barnyard knows.
And you'll come back, come back, come back—
They always do—in ten years or a score
And find this pig-sty for your pig's broad back,
And in it all religion, literature, art—
I know, I know the secret of your heart.

Drink up, drink up, the troughs in Paris and
London are no better than your own,
Joyce learned that bitterly in a foreign land.
Don't laugh, there is no answer to that one!
Outside this pig-sty life deteriorates,
Civilisation dwindles. We are the last preserve
Of Eden in a world of savage states.
With a touch more cunning and a touch more nerve
You'd establish at the trough your own good place;
Meet all the finest sows if you would just
Not damn each hog you meet straight to his face;
They're all your friends if you but knew. Please put
Your skyward turned snout unto the ground
And nuts that Africa never knew you'll find.

Remember Colum and his fair-green promise,
Young maidens' laughter on a midland lane
A greater singer far than Dylan Thomas
Phrase-maker innocent as April rain.
And see O'Casey lost in English Devon
Who never wrote another line worth reading
Since he left St. George's Pocket in 'twenty-seven
Weaving in vain an alien material.
The blue and rapturous phrase, the brave banner
Of a man's own people shabby and torn
Strained on the thorn of the English manner
Lost is the man who thinks that he can scorn
His parish mother's paps. The greatest sage
May not reject his people's heritage.

Around you, don't forget is genius which
Walks with feet rooted in the native soil
Don't sweep them from your path or say that such
Are merely drunken talkers without mind.
The poet's task is not to solve the riddle
Of Man and God but buckleap on a door
And grab his screeching female by her middle
To the music of a melodeon (preferably), roar
Against the Western waves of Connemara
Up lads and thrash the beetles. This tradition
Is what the stranger comes to buy or borrow
What you would leave to chase a worthless mission.
Leave Christ and Christlike problems and you'll be
The synthesis of Gaelic poetry.

I went away and thought of all the answers
But there were none that killed his ghastly smile
Which said to me: life has no enchantment,
Art is no more than Sancho Panza's Isle;
A phrase made up to crown a pint of beer,
A paragraph for a gossip columnist,
A group of idle men and women or
Anything temporary, sensationalist—
Shakespeare and Blake, where are they now, or Keats?
Drink up your drinks, get yourself a job . . .

O God, I cried, these treats are not the treats
That Heaven offers in the Golden Cup.
And I heard the demon's terrifying yell:
There is no place as perfect as our hell.

Subject — Denouncing those writers
who left Ireland because
when they left their writing
deteriorated.
Ireland is where you get sources for
your writing.
Depending living in Ireland.

BANK HOLIDAY

NINETEEN fifty was the year
The August Bank Holiday that I am here
Sitting in my room alone
Conscious of a season gone;
Ultimate failure straggling up
Through the barren daydream crop.
I must not defer a date
For a meeting with my fate.

There he comes your alter ego
Past the Waterloo and Searson's
With a silly gaping mouth
Sucking smiles from every slut,
Sure that this is Heaven's high manna—
God is good to Patrick Kavanagh,
Building like a rejected lover
Dust into an ivory tower.

In the pubs for seven years
Men have given him their ears,
Buying the essence of his heart
With a porter-perfumed fart.
Make him turn his pockets out
And his seven harvests count.
Spread out the vain collection—
Not a penny of affection.

Knock him to the ground for he
Is your sister Vanity,
If your brother Clown
Exhibited for a sneering town.
He's your son who's named Tomorrow,
Kill him, kill Remorse your mother,
Be the father of your fate
On this nineteen fifty date.

A SIMPLE man arrived in town,
Lover of letters; more than that
A true believer in the mystical
Power of poets. Moral, yet
Willing for a well-made song
To let the poet choose his own.

The fruit would justify the rape
Of blossoms, though he might regret
The virgin pink of May—
And thus he came to get
A peep into the temple of
The Muses. He was full of love.

A bearded man who wore a cloak
He sighted. To himself, he said,
This is my man. He introduced
His plan. The bearded man replied,
I'll lead you through the world of art
Where beats a universal heart.

SCENE:

This is the entrance to the bohemian jungle which lies on the perimeter of Commerce.

From the depths of the rotten vegetation can be heard the screams of drunken girls.

The gabble from Schools of Acting, Painting, Music.

A stream of large cars passes in.

In one of these cars sits Count O'Mulligan, wealthy father of Sheila O'Mulligan, the star of 'Cardinal Error'.

Count O'Mulligan brings with him two gross of gold, diamond-studded replicas of the Ardagh Chalice as Cups to be competed for at the Drama Festival.

Above the stinking weeds, whose life is derived from the moonlight, rises the phallic tower of Bohemia's temple, The Theatre.

The Catholic Cultural League in procession headed by its Chaplain, Father John, who is loaded down with two gross of rosary beads for presentation to the performers, moves slowly through.

The fantasy reminds the Countryman of the nighttown scene in *Ulysses*, or Dante's Hell or something out of John Bunyan.

Through the railings is visible an apartment in which a wild bottle party is in progress. Young women are being led from the main room into bedrooms. One of these girls the Countryman recognises as the highly—as he imagined—respectable daughter of a highly respectable doctor.

In the foyers of several theatres can be seen a number of early middle-aged women who are talking about actors and musicians while trying to sow a catch-crop of passion in this favourable climate.

Other sights are: politicians carrying flags, the women correspondents of several newspapers, radio commentators, the President of the Travel Society. This man is showing some Americans around and explaining to them that Necessity Number One is not unavailable in this country. Snatches of the conversation came over:

> *American:*
> If there's no Sex, what good is my shillelagh?

> *Travelman:*
> The situation is improving daily.

> *Guide:*
> Here's where we go in—
> Throw it away, throw it away, throw it away.

> *Countryman:*
> Throw what away?

> *Guide:*
> The cold disgust upon your face,
> The Ussherine Refusal,
> The cut-and-dried opinions—
> See life as just amusing.

> See life as newspapers show it
> Without a moral judgement,
> The bank Integrity
> Holds but a beggar's lodgement.

Truth's what's in power to-day,
The lie's what's in the breadline
So take you Gospel straight
From the morning headline.

Bow down to fools in office,
Keep yourself in practice,
Admire the successful,
But damn the between rackets.

Anticipate the failure,
His smile when out of place
Can blast your life. Have no
Memory for Failure's face.

Simply reverse the manner
By which you've lived till now;
Life is not a heifer
But a great-uddered cow.

They join the bottle-party where there is a constant shuffling and poking
of heads through the crowd as if everyone wanted to speak to someone else.

Countryman:
Show me some authors.

Guide:
You saw the look they gave you, that was you
Being their conscience
Hide that mirror,
Have a drink.
(To barman) Mick,
A ball.
(To a man) How is Des?

Countryman:
You know them all.
Have I to go through all this to find
The world of Art?

Guide:
For success, yes.
They will not accept
The man not broken and remade
To the formula.
The real is too unpredictable.
Have another drink . . .
Mick!

Countryman:
This is a wonderful world.
(To a girl half-tight)
How about me kissing you?

Before he has time to organise his courage there is a commotion near the
door as the crowd rushes forward to catch a glimpse as Father John, Chaplain
to the c.c.l., passing by with Sheila O'Mulligan on his arm.

Guide:
She's the Adjudicator at the Festival.

Countryman:
She looks a good thing.
There's something to be said for the common bitch,
She has not virtue's jealous-gripping power
Such
As the good woman who can devour
A man's mind and entrails, spit
His chewed-up personality out on to the grass
While her hungry thought goes screaming, howling wildly
For a soul, a soul to fill a gaping space.
For here is the stuffed tiger of Desire
With nylon fur and wire-recorded roar
The flashing fangs like Instinct's, yet quite safe,
Quite safe . . .
And what a bore!

Angry faces are turned in the speaker's direction. A young man with a
frustrated grin, seizes the Countryman by the shoulder.

The Man:
Sheila's performance in 'Cardinal Error' was aesthetic
The Catholic World by its readers' vote
Acclaimed her outstanding Catholic of the year . . .
So if you want your dial defaced—

Guide returns and explains that Countryman is a friend of his.

Countryman:
A thug!

Girl (whom he had tried to kiss):
Well, Jack's a friend of mine. See?
Come on, Jack, the curtain's going up;
Mummie's too tight to leave the (appropriate word) car.
Who was that bullock in the china-shop?

The Guide leads the Countryman out to get sick. Around them they see
bodies in varying states of futile lechery. The President of the Travel Society
and the American are judging a Beauty Competition. A woman reporter is
present eagerly listening.

Travelman:
How do girls here compare . . . ?

The Guide and the Countryman move away to where Count O'Mulligan is
standing talking to Father John.

Father John:
This is the great Art patron, Count O'Mulligan,
Sheila's father, the motor salesman.
Who's your friend?

Guide:
A man from the mythical land of Simple Country
Learning about life, about Art.

Chaplain:
Has he a grudge against life?
Why is he so sour?

Guide:
He is difficult, he sees life as morning in a field of dewy grass.
He is shocked at the corruption through which all must pass
To arrive at knowledge
He will not take the world as it runs
I fear he will suffer for his denial
Of what Is.

Guide follows Countryman who has moved away.

Guide:
Why did you insult the great O'Mulligan?
Richest man in town, worth knowing.

Countryman:
I know him;
He once employed a poet in his factory
At thirty bob a week
And gave ten thousand pounds to the C.C.L.
He has never committed rape or bigamy it is true
Goes to Mass every morning in fact,
A good beginning to the businessman's day
God nicely in His place, card-indexed,
His stomach comfortable on golf dreams
The Bishop calling round to have dinner to discuss
With him the problem of the city's poor.
A charitable man is Count O'Mulligan
Chairman of the Christian Beggars' Guild
Benign, bountiful—evil.

There is further commotion as the Players made up for the verse-play
pass by.

Countryman (musingly)*:*
Sorcerers,
Mediaeval monks,
Ancient Abbesses,
Necromancers,
Alchemists.

Guide:
Culture on the march, join in.
Oh, here's the Count again.
Be nice to him.

The Count:
The greatest of the Arts is music—
Mozart, Beethoven, Kreisler, Menuhin;
After music, the art of the actor—
Olivier, Crosby, Barry, Ireland's droll—

Chaplain:
And McCormick, Ireland's soul.

Newspaper photographers push Guide and Countryman aside to get shots
of the Count and Father John. They interview Sheila O'Mulligan.

Interviewers:
What's your opinion of the atomic bomb?
Should it be outlawed by the United Nations?
What is the future of the film industry?
Will Television pay still higher wages?
What's your opinion of the American Theatre?
Who is America's outstanding mind?
What is your message to the Irish people?
Are we still the spiritual leaders of mankind?
Is religion still the force in Filmland?
Did the Cleaner Films and Rosary Crusade
Bring further customers to the Cinema?

Countryman:
O God! O God! O God!

Guide:
This is the world of Art,
Of Love.
You dream of romantic sin, the Seven
Are the locked doors of the idealistic Heaven.

Countryman:
I dreamt of sin and it was fire
A May-time-in-the-fields desire,
Violent, exciting, new,
Whin-blossoms burning up the dew;
Sudden death and sudden birth
Among the hierarchies of the earth;
Kings that ruled with absolute power
If 'twas only for an hour;
Trees were green, mountains sheer
And God dramatically clear.
But here in this nondescript land
Everything is secondhand:
Nothing ardently growing,
Nothing, coming, nothing going,
Tepid fevers, nothing hot,
None alive enough to rot;
Nothing clearly defined . . .
Every head is challenged. Friend,
This is hell you've brought me to.
Where's the gate that we came through?

Guide:
Simply imagine the nightmare's ended,
And you're already outside the gate
Watching the patrons, players, playboys
Worshipping the second-rate.
That's Hell's secret, to be the mirror
For a mixture of truth and error.

At this point the satire explodes in a burst of wild cheering as the Country-
man joins a group of Crumlin gurriers who are betting on a competition for
who can urinate the highest. The Countryman wins, but is later arrested
and charged with committing a public nuisance.

IRISH STEW

OUR ancient civilisation—and—
This Christian State of Ireland!

He said to open his oration
With protective incantation.

Then, all in the Name of God
He turned on me a beaming broad

Face that twitched with a restive hate,
And this is what that man did state:

You're far too great a genius to
Talk of steak and onions or a stew,

Luxury would ruin your sublime
Imagination in no time.

And domesticity, wife, house, car,
We want you always as you are.

Such things don't fit into the scheme
Of one who dreams the poet's dream.

Your wildness is your great attraction,
You could not be a man of action.

Now, you'll never have to worry how to live—
A man who has so much to give.

My cousin dabbles in verse? but he
Has not your spark of poetry;

Unlike you he has not nobly strained—
But in economics he is trained;

He has a politician's mind
To deal with an ugly world designed;

Knows how to handle you great men,
Artists and masters of the pen,

Can run an office, plan a series
Of lectures for the Cork O'Learys

Or Jesuits of Clongowes College
Because he's got the practical knowledge

And that is why he has been sent
To travel on the Continent

To bring back the secret of great arts
To Kerry and remoter parts.

To spread in Naas and Clonakilty
News of Gigli and R. H. Rilke.

Our last art emissary whored
And that's one reason we can't afford

To risk an important man like you
In the dangerous European stew.

THE CHRISTMAS MUMMERS

Apology

THIS is the stuff of which I was made,
The crude loud homespun bagging at the knees,
The primitive but not simple barbarities,
The casual labourer with an unskilful spade.
Unsimple ignorance was our only trade;
Our minds untrained to tensions would not seize
The string and stretch it till sincerity's
Tune to the pain-nobled end was played.
We shouted on mountains, but no god gathered
The wise sayings and the extraordinarily pure notes;
All went for nothing, a whole nation blathered
Without art, which is Character's city name.
And that is the story, the reason for the trailing coats;
The unmannerly bravado is the bluff of shame.

The Roomer

Room, room my gallant boys and give us room to rhyme,
We'll show you some activity coming on this Christmastime;
We act the rich, we act the poor, the simple and the critical,
We act the scenes that lie behind the public and political
We bring you noble statesmen and poets loused with song
And actors who make stacks of money making fun,
And if you don't believe me and give in to what I say
I'll call in Seamus O'Donavan and he'll soon clear the way.

Seamus O'Donavan

Here comes I Seamus O'Donavan—against the British menace
I fought when I was younger in the War of Independence;
Encouraged the national language, too old myself to learn it—
And if I got a pension who says I didn't earn it?
In days when 'The Emergency' was no poor cow in labour
But war most awful threatening the world and our neighbour
I took my musket down and joined young men who were no moochers
But soldiering nobly for the land into congenial futures;
My face as you can see is clear-marked old ITA,

An Irish face good-natured, Catholic, liberal and gay
My hair is turning whitish (though in youth severely mauled,
Oddly, no man who ever fought for Ireland goes quite bald).
For the good name of my country I am most insanely zealous
And of comrades who got richer I am not the least bit jealous
And if you don't believe me and give in to what I say
I'll call in a Successful Statesman and he'll soon clear the way.

Successful Statesman
Here comes I a Successful Statesman, from the people I am sprung
My father a National Teacher learned in Gaelic rune and song;
My mother was of ancient stock and early taught to me
The fear of God and daily toil and common poverty.
By the worthy Christian Brothers my character was shaped
And we prayed for Mother Erin when by Saxons she was raped;
I played my part in the struggle—played football for my county
And won an All-Ireland medal when I was barely twenty.
And I never deserted poetry—God be good to poor Owen Roe!
And the thousand Kerry poets who were slaughtered by the foe.
And if you don't believe me and give in to what I say
I'll call in Sean Og O'Gum and he'll soon clear the way.

Sean Og O'Gum
Here comes I Sean Og O'Gum, seven pounds have I
Retainer from the Government for writing poetry:
I write about tinker tribes and porter-drinking men
Who shoulder-shove their minds into the handle of my pen.
The clans are scything song again on rebel-ripened hills
And reason screams for mercy at the stratching of our quills.
We know a hundred thousand ways for saying 'Drink your liquor'
When we toss the coin of language ne'er a ha'penny comes a sticker.
No truck have we with pagans or the foreign-backside licker.
I set my boat's proud prow to sea and hoist my ballad sails
And chant on decks of destiny for the all-too-silent Gaels
And if you don't believe me and give in to what I say
I'll call in a Famous Actor and he'll soon clear the way.

Famous Actor
Here comes I, a Famous Actor of films stage and radio,
I was born the son of a peasant in the county of Mayo;

I am the man they call on to speak the verse of Sean
And other Gaelic poets, and lately I have done
A lot of work in English that's well out of the groove—
The popular taste in culture we are aiming to improve;
And last week when adjudicating at a Drama Festival,
I found that Irish audiences liked Eliot best of all.
I've escaped the grind of daily toil and cabins dirty, smelly
And I'm married to the daughter of Senator O'Kelly,
And if you don't believe me and give in to what I say
I'll call in Senator O'Kelly and he'll soon clear the way.

Senator O'Kelly
Here comes I Senator O'Kelly a simple businessman,
I make no claims to culture though I do the best I can
To foster our great artists and though business presses so
I go to exhibitions and I spend a lot of dough.
And one thing most I do regret, a thing to me most shocking
And that is certain critics who are far too fond of knocking
The men who make their country known throughout the artistic sphere
Earning dollars with the pictures at which these fellows sneer.
As a common or garden businessman this attitude I deplore
But I thank God for our vigilant Press which shuts on them its door.
And if you don't believe me and give in to what I say
I'll call in a Leading Editor and he'll soon clear the way.

Leading Editor
Here comes I a Leading Editor who knows the Irish dream,
I'm open to every idea that fits in with the regime:
The Liberal Opposition who complain of bishops' mitres
And the rising cost of turnips and the censorship on writers.
The Press is free, the radio gives them a free debate,
New Statesmanism is essential to every well-run state.
These are not Lilliputian cranks as destructive critics scream
They are the Official Liberal Opposition and part of the regime.
And if you don't believe me and give in to what I say
Go to the bogs or Birmingham or Mountjoy right away.

EXPLANATION:
The custom of Mummers or rhymers going around before Christmas performing
in rural kitchens still lives on in some parts of Ireland. Each Mummer re-presents some
historical or nonsensical character. The formula is exactly as in this piece.

The Hitler war was known officially in Southern Ireland as 'The Emergency'.

Owen Roe. Owen Roe Sullivan was in the front rank of the ten thousand Irish poets of his day. The standing army of Irish poets seldom falls below this figure.

Football prowess in Ireland, as in Hungary today, has always been a path to political success.

Contrived, manufactured verse with its necessary lack of any passionate impulse or belief is what passed for poetry among the Gaels. Phrase-making. The poet was a romantically wild man who was seldom sober, was a devil for the women. Dylan Thomas brought this bogusity to the English who thought it new and wonderful.

New Statesmanism. The *New Statesman* is the name of an English radical weekly.

Mountjoy is the principal Dublin jail.

Working on the turf bogs in Ireland is equivalent to salt-mining in Siberia.

The surplus Irish population who cannot get into the B.B.C. work in Birmingham where they are to be seen high up in the sky painting gasometers.

TALE OF TWO CITIES

THE streets of London are not paved with gold,
The streets of London are paved with failures;
They get up and move about when they are filled with drink
Just as in Dublin. Yesterday in Fleet Street
In a pub I met one. He shook my hand
And he was full of poisonous fellowship as he looked into my eyes:
I would have a double whiskey.
I was from Dublin, most wonderful spot on earth.

How was Harry Kelly, Jack Sullivan and Brady
And Galligan the greatest Dubliner of them all?
I'll tell you the name of the greatest living poet, he muttered,
He lives near Manchester and will be heard of yet.
What about Auden, I interrupted. He ignored me—
Yeats was second-rate, not a patch on Higgins—
I was back in Dublin as I listened.
You certainly must have another double whiskey, he cried
And once again he gripped my hand in his
And said there was no place like Dublin.
His friendship wounded, but I dare not complain
For that would seem boorish. Yet it was this
Insincere good-nature that hurt me in Dublin.
The sardonic humour of a man about to be hanged.
But London would not hang him; it laid him horizontal
To dream of the books he had written in liquor
Once again he would return to Dublin.
Where among the failures he would pass unnoticed,
Happy in pubs talking about yesterday's wits,
And George Moore's use of the semi-colon.

O COME all ye tragic poets and sing a stave with me—
Give over T. S. Eliot and also W. B.
We'll sing our way through Stephen's Green where March has never found
In the growing grass a cadence of the verse of Ezra Pound.

The University girls are like tulip bulbs behind
More luxurious than ever from Holland was consigned,
Those bulbs will shortly break in flower—rayon, silk and cotton
And our verbal constipation will be totally forgotten.

Philosophy's graveyard—only dead men analyse
The reason for existence. Come all you solemn boys
From out your dictionary world and literary gloom—
Kafka's mad, Picasso's sad in Despair's confining room.

O come all darling poets and try to look more happy,
Forget about sexology as you gossip in the cafe;
Forget about the books you've read and the inbred verses there
Forget about the Kinsey Report and take a mouthful of air.

The world began this morning, God-dreamt and full of birds,
The fashion shops were glorious with the new collection of words.
And Love was practising phrases in young balladry—
Ten thousand years must pass before the birth of Psychology.

O come all ye gallant poets—to know it doesn't matter
Is imagination's message—break out but do not scatter.
Ordinary things wear lovely wings—the peacock's body's common.
O come all ye youthful poets and try to be more human.

WHO KILLED JAMES JOYCE?

Who killed James Joyce?
I, said the commentator,
I killed James Joyce
For my graduation.

What weapon was used
To slay mighty Ulysses?
The weapon that was used
Was a Harvard thesis.

How did you bury Joyce?
In a broadcast symposium.
That's how we buried Joyce
To a tuneful encomium.   *warm o high praise*

Who carried the coffin out?
Six Dublin codgers
Led into Langham Place
By W. R. Rodgers.

Who said the burial prayers?—
Please do not hurt me—
Joyce was no Protestant,
Surely not Bertie?

Who killed Finnegan?
I, said a Yale-man,
I was the man who made
The corpse for the wake man.

And did you get high marks,
The Ph.D.?
I got the B.Litt.
And my master's degree.

Did you get money
For your Joycean knowledge?
I got a scholarship
To Trinity College.

I made the pilgrimage
In the Bloomsday swelter
From the Martello Tower
To the cabby's shelter.

HOUSE PARTY TO CELEBRATE
THE DESTRUCTION OF THE ROMAN CATHOLIC
CHURCH IN IRELAND

HER book was out, and did she devastate
The Roman Catholic Church on every page!
And in Seamus's house they met to celebrate
With giggles high the dying monster's rage.

When Seamus gazed upon this woman he
Reflected on one absolute disgrace
Outside the bounds of every decency—
'A female replica of Cromwell's face'

Was how some rural savage had described
This noble woman—she was not blotched
Her wart was a beauty mole. He had been bribed
To rhyme his sneer. Some Bishop had been touched.

So terrible was Seamus's emotion
The sherry glass was dancing in his hand—
The Jansenistic priesthood of the nation
Had perished by this woman writer's hand.

With fighting admiration in his eyes
He could not see his wife but only Her
He stammered: 'You did more than satirise.
Great artist! The Irish Voltaire.'

The reviews were coming in by every post
Warm and fulsome—Seamus read extracts:
'The Roman Catholic Hierarchy must
Be purple now with rage. She states the facts

With wit, and wit is what they cannot bear'.
In far off parishes of Cork and Kerry
Old priests walked homeless in the winter air
As Seamus poured another pale dry sherry.

THE fabled daughters of memory are all pastiche,
God born-clean we desire;
But thoughts are sin and words are soiled
And Nietzschean blood is syphilitic.

The children take delight in levelling the city,
Violently tear down the walls,
Screeching from the steps of a ruin
Where a broken milk bottle rolls.

PORTRAIT OF THE ARTIST

I NEVER lived, I have no history,
I deserted no wife to take another,
I rotted in a room and leave—this message.

The morning newspapers and the radio
Announced his death in a few horrid words:
—A man of talent who lacked the little more
That makes the difference
Between success and failure.
The biographer turned away disgusted from
A theme that had no plot
And wrote instead the life of Reilly.

Great artist, came to town at twenty-one.
Took a job,
Threw it up,
Lived a year with Mrs. Brown.

Wrote a play,
Got the pox,
Made a film,
Wrote the incidental music.

Left his Mrs.
Took another,
Lived in Paris
With a mummer.

His critics were
Denounced as monsters,
Jungle beasts
Who hated Art.

Great artist, great man, the pattern was perfect
And the biographer recorded it with enthusiasm.

THERE'S nothing happening that you hate
That's really worthwhile slamming;
Be patient. If you only wait
You'll see time gently damning

Newspaper bedlamites who raised
Each day the devil's howl
Versifiers who had seized
The poet's begging bowl

The whole hysterical passing show
The hour apotheosised
Into a cul-de-sac will go
And be not even despised.

I

AUDITORS IN

I

THE problem that confronts me here
Is to be eloquent yet sincere;
Let myself rip and not go phoney
In an inflated testimony.
Is verse an entertainment only?
Or is it a profound and holy
Faith that cries the inner history
Of the failure of man's mission?
Should it be my job to mention
Precisely how I chanced to fail
Through a cursed ideal.
Write down here: he knew what he wanted—
Evilest knowledge ever haunted
Man when he can picture clear
Just what he is searching for.

A car, a big suburban house,
Half secret that he might not lose
The wild attraction of the poor
But proud, the fanatic lure
For women of the poet's way
And diabolic underlay;

The gun of pride can bring them down
At twenty paces in the town—
For what? the tragedy is this
Pride's gunman hesitates to kiss:
A romantic Rasputin
Praying at the heart of sin.

He cannot differentiate
Say if he does not want to take
From moral motives or because
Nature has ideal in her laws.

But to get down to the factual—
You are not homosexual.
And yet you live without a wife,
A most disorganised sort of life.
You've not even bred illegitimates
A lonely lecher whom the fates
By a financial trick castrates.

You're capable of an intense
Love that is experience.
Remember how your heart was moved
And youth's eternity was proved
When you saw a young girl going to Mass
On a weekday morning as
You yourself used to go

Down to church from Ednamo.
Your imagination still enthuses
Over the dandelions at Willie Hughes'
And these are equally valid
For urban epic, a peasant ballad.
Not mere memory but the Real
Poised in the poet's commonweal.
And you must take yourself in hand
And dig and ditch your authentic land.

Wake up, wake up and compromise
On the non-essential sides
Love's round you in a rapturous bevy
But you are bankrupt by the levy
Imposed upon the ideal:
Her Cheshire-cat smile surmounts the wall.
She smiles 'Wolf, wolf, come be my lover'
Unreal you find and yet you never
Catch on. One cannot but feel sorry,
For the ideal is purgatory.

Yet do not be too much dismayed
It's on your hand, the humble trade
Of versing that can easily
Restore your equanimity
And lay the looney ghosts that goad
The savages of Pembroke Road . . .
Bow down here and thank your God.

II

After the prayer I am ready to enter my heart
Indifferent to the props of a reputation:
Some feeble sallies of a peasant plantation,
The rotten shafts of a remembered cart
Holding up the conscious crust of art.
No quiet corner here for contemplation,
No roots of faith to give an angry passion
Validity. I at the bottom will start
Try to ignore the shame-reflecting eyes
Of worshippers who made their god too tall
To share their food or do the non-stupendous,
They gave him for exploring empty skies
Instead of a little room where he might write for
Men too real to live by vapid legends.

Away, away away on wings like Joyce's
Mother Earth is putting my brand new clothes in order
Praying, she says, that I no more ignore her
Yellow buttons she found in fields at bargain prices.
Kelly's Big Bush for a button-hole. Surprises
In every pocket—the stress at Connolly's corner
Myself at Annavackey on Armagh border
Or calm and collected in a calving crisis.
Not sad at all as I float away away
With Mother keeping me to the vernacular.
I have a home to return to now. O blessing
For the Return in Departure. Somewhere to stay
Doesn't matter. What is distressing
Is walking eagerly to go nowhere in particular.

From the sour soil of a town where all roots canker
I turn away to where the Self reposes
The placeless Heaven that's under all our noses
Where we're shut off from all the barren anger
No time for self-pitying melodrama
A million Instincts know no other uses
Than all day long to feed and charm the Muses
Till they become pure positive. O hunger
Where all have mouths of desire and none
Is willing to be eaten: I am so glad
To come accidentally upon
My self at the end of a tortuous road
And have learned with surprise that God
Unworshipped withers to the Futile One.

INNOCENCE

THEY laughed at one I loved—
The triangular hill that hung
Under the Big Forth. They said
That I was bounded by the whitethorn hedges
Of the little farm and did not know the world.
But I knew that love's doorway to life
Is the same doorway everywhere.

Ashamed of what I loved
I flung her from me and called her a ditch
Although she was smiling at me with violets.

But now I am back in her briary arms
The dew of an Indian Summer morning lies
On bleached potato-stalks—
What age am I?

I do not know what age I am,
I am no mortal age;
I know nothing of women,
Nothing of cities,
I cannot die
Unless I walk outside these whitethorn hedges.

SHE kicked a pebble with her toe,
She tapped a railing idly—
And when we met she swerved and took
The corner very widely.
I though, that could be love; I know
The power of the male,
But without an introduction
The thing, she knows, will fail.

And so I planned for many a day
A ruse to soothe convention:
Stare up at numbers over doors
And some doctor mention;
Or get myself invited to
Some party where she'd be—
But all these things went down the drain
Of anti-dignity.

And then one day we actually
Did meet by introduction
And I told her with a laugh or two
She had been my distraction.

ANTE-NATAL DREAM

I ONLY know that I was there
With hayseed in my hair
Lying on the shady side
Of a haycock in July.

describing relation with Nature.

A crowd was pressing round
My body on the ground
Prising the lids of my eyes—
Open and you'll be wise.

The sky that roared with bees,
The row of poplar trees
Along the stream struck deep
And would not let me sleep.

A boortree tried hard to
Let me see it grow,
Mere notice was enough,
She would take care of love.

A clump of nettles cried:
We'll saturate your pride
Till you are oozing with
The richness of our myth;

For we are all you'll know
No matter where you go—
Every insect, weed
Kept singing in my head.

Thistle, ragwort, bluebottle,
Cleg that maddens cattle
Were crowding round me there
With hayseed in my hair.

TO BE DEAD

To BE dead is to stop believing in
The masterpieces we will begin tomorrow;
To be an exile is to be a coward,
To know that growth has stopped,
That whatever is done is the end;
Correct the proofs over and over,
Rewrite old poems again and again,
Tell lies to yourself about your achievement:
Ten printed books on the shelves.
Though you know that no one loves you for
   what you have done,
But for what you might do.

And you perhaps, take up religion bitterly
Which you laughed at in your youth,
Well not actually laughed
But it wasn't your kind of truth.

PRELUDE

GIVE us another poem, he said
Or they will think your muse is dead;
Another middle-age departure
Of Apollo from the trade of archer.
Bring out a book as soon as you can
To let them see you're a living man,
Whose comic spirit is untamed
Though sadness for a little claimed
The precedence; and tentative
You pulled your punch and wondered if
Old Cunning Silence might not be
A better bet than poetry.

You have not got the countenance
To hold the angle of pretence,
That angry bitter look for one
Who knows that art's a kind of fun;
That all true poems laugh inwardly
Out of grief-born intensity.
Dullness alone can get you beat
And so can humour's counterfeit.
You have not got a chance with fraud
And might as well be true to God.

Then link your laughter out of doors
In sunlight past the sick-faced whores
Who chant the praise of love that isn't
And bring their bastards to be Christened
At phoney founts by bogus priests
With rites mugged up by journalists
Walk past professors looking serious
Fondling an unpublished thesis—
'A child! my child! my darling son'
Some Poets of Nineteen Hundred and One.

Note well the face profoundly grave,
An empty mind can house a knave.
Be careful to show no defiance,
They've made pretence into a science;
Card-sharpers of the art committee
Working all the provincial cities,
They cry 'Eccentric' if they hear
A voice that seems at all sincere.
Fold up their table and their gear
And with the money disappear.

But satire is unfruitful prayer,
Only wild shoots of pity there,
And you must go inland and be
Lost in compassion's ecstasy,
Where suffering soars in summer air—
The millstone has become a star.

Count then your blessings, hold in mind
All that has loved you or been kind:
Those women on their mercy missions,
Rescue work with kiss or kitchens,
Perceiving through the comic veil
The poet's spirit in travail.
Gather the bits of road that were
Not gravel to the traveller
But eternal lanes of joy
On which no man who walks can die.
Bring in the particular trees
That caught you in their mysteries,
And love again the weeds that grew
Somewhere specially for you.
Collect the river and the stream
That flashed upon a pensive theme,
And a positive world make,
A world man's world cannot shake.
And do not lose love's resolution
Though face to face with destitution.

If Platitude should claim a place
Do not denounce his humble face;
His sentiments are well intentioned
He has a part in the larger legend.

So now my gentle tiger burning
In the forest of no-yearning
Walk on serenely, do not mind
That Promised Land you thought to find,
Where the worldly-wise and rich take over
The mundane problems of the lower,
Ignore Power's schismatic sect,
Lovers alone lovers protect.

LIKE Achilles you had a goddess for mother,
For only the half-god can see
The immortal in things mortal;
The far-frightened surprise in a crow's flight
Or the moonlight
That stays for ever in a tree.

In stubble fields the ghosts of corn are
The important spirits that imagination heeds.
Nothing dies; there are no empty
Spaces in the cleanest-reaped fields.

It was no human weakness when you flung
Your body prostrate on a cabbage drill—
Heart-broken with Priam for Hector ravaged;
You did not know why you cried,
This was the night he died—
Most wonderful-horrible
October evening among those cabbages.

The intensity that radiated from
The Far Field Rock—you afterwards denied—
Was the half-god seeing his half-brothers
Joking on the fabulous mountain-side.

KERR'S ASS

WE BORROWED the loan of Kerr's big ass
To go to Dundalk with butter,
Brought him home the evening before the market
An exile that night in Mucker.

We heeled up the cart before the door,
We took the harness inside—
The straw-stuffed straddle, the broken breeching
With bits of bull-wire tied;

The winkers that had no choke-band,
The collar and the reins . . .
In Ealing Broadway, London Town
I name their several names

Until a world comes to life—
Morning, the silent bog,
And the God of imagination waking
In a Mucker fog.

EPIC

I HAVE lived in important places, times
When great events were decided, who owned
That half a rood of rock, a no-man's land
Surrounded by our pitchfork-armed claims.
I heard the Duffys shouting 'Damn your soul'
And old McCabe stripped to the waist, seen
Step the plot defying blue cast-steel—
'Here is the march along these iron stones'
That was the year of the Munich bother. Which
Was more important? I inclined
To lose my faith in Ballyrush and Gortin
Till Homer's ghost came whispering to my mind
He said: I made the Iliad from such
A local row. Gods make their own importance.

ON READING A BOOK ON COMMON
WILD FLOWERS

O THE prickly sow thistle that grew in the hollow of the Near Field
I used it as a high jump coming home in the evening—
A hurdle race over the puce blossoms of the sow thistles.
Am I late?
Am I tired?
Is my heart sealed
From the ravening passion that will eat it out
Till there is not one pure moment left?

O the greater fleabane that grew at the back of the potato pit:
I often trampled through it looking for rabbit burrows!
The burnet saxifrage was there in profusion
And the autumn gentian—
I knew them all by eyesight long before I knew their names.
We were in love before we were introduced.

Let me not moralize or have remorse, for these names
Purify a corner of my mind;
I jump over them and rub them with my hands,
And a free moment appears brand new and spacious
Where I may live beyond the reach of desire.

I HAD A FUTURE

O I HAD a future
A future.

Gods of the imagination bring back to life
The personality of those streets,
Not any streets
But the streets of nineteen forty.

Give the quarter-seeing eyes I looked out of
The animal-remembering mind
The fog through which I walked towards
        The mirage
That was my future.

The women I was to meet
They were nowhere within sight.

And then the pathos of the blind soul,
How without knowing stands in its own
        kingdom.
Bring me a small detail
How I felt about money,
Not frantic as later,
There was the future.

Show me the stretcher-bed I slept on
In a room on Drumcondra Road,
Let John Betjeman call for me in a car.

It is summer and the eerie beat
Of madness in Europe trembles the
Wings of the butterflies along the canal.

O I had a future.

THE ROWLEY MILE

As I was walking down a street
Upon a summer's day
A typical girl I chanced to meet
And gathered courage to say:
'I've seen you many, many times
Upon this Rowley Mile
And I'm foolish enough to believe you love
Me for you always smile'.

Well, she gathered herself into a ball
Receding all the time.
She said: 'I beg your pardon,
I do not know what you mean'.
I stammered vainly for the right word
I said: 'I mean to say
I'm not trying to get off with you
Or anything in that way'.

The street was full of eyes that stared
At something very odd.
I tried to imagine how little means
Such a contretemps to God.
I followed her a few slow yards
'Please just one moment stop'
And then I dashed with urgent tread
Into a corner shop.

As I walked down that sunny street
I was a broken man
Thanks to an Irish girl
Who smiles but is true to the plan
Taught her by Old Gummy Granny—
You must try out your power with a smile,
But come to the test hard reality must
Make the pace on the Rowley Mile.

THE birds sang in the wet trees
And as I listened to them it was a hundred years from now
And I was dead and someone else was listening to them.
But I was glad I had recorded for him
    The melancholy.

THE HERO

HE WAS an ordinary man, a man full of humour,
Born for no high sacrifice, to be no marble god;
But all the gods had failed that harvest and someone
    spread the rumour
That he might be deluded into taking on the job.
And they came to him in the spring
And said: you are our poet-king.

Their evil weakness smiled on him and he had no
    answer to it,
They drove him out of corners into the public gaze;
And the more he tried to defend himself the more they
    cried, O poet
Why must you always insult us when we only want to praise?
And he said: I wish you would
Pick on someone else to be your god.

They laughed when he told them he had no intention of
    dying
For virtue of truth—that his ideal would be
As a mediaeval Sultan, in a middle-class setting enjoying
Many female slaves—where Luxury,
All joyful mysteries,
Takes Wisdom on her knees.

Thinking of the mean reality of middle-class life
They saw the normal as outlandish joy
And all of them embittered with a second-hand wife,
Growing literary, begged him to die
Before his vision become
The slightest bit tame.

He advised them that gods are invisibly cloaked by a crowd,
Mortality touches the conspicuous;
They had the wrong ideas of a god
Who once all known becomes ridiculous.
—I am as obvious as an auctioneer
Dreaming of twenty thousand pounds a year.

At this they roared in the streets and became quite
    hysterical
And he knew he was the cause of this noise—
Yet he had acted reasonably, had performed no miracle,
Had spoken in a conventional voice,
And he said: surely you can
See that I am an ordinary man?

But instead they rushed off and published in all the
    papers
And magazines the photograph of their poet genius, god;
And all the cafés buzzed with his outrageous sayings—
He feared he was beaten and might have to take the job
For one day in the insincere city
He had an attack of self-pity.

He looked in the shoe-shop windows where all the shoes
    were toys.
Everything else similarly scaled down;
The hotels were doll's houses of doll's vice—
He was trapped in a pygmy town.
Vainly on all fours
He tried the small doors.

Crowds of little men went in with smooth authority
To settle this and that at boardroom tables;
Sometimes they looked up and imagined him Morality,
The silenced bishop of some heathen fables,
The ruler of the See
Of monstrous Anarchy.

Yet he found out at last the nature and the cause
Of what was and is and he no more wanted
To avoid the ludicrous cheer, the sick applause—
The sword of satire in his hand became blunted,
And for the insincere city
He felt a profound pity.

IF EVER you go to Dublin town
In a hundred years or so
Inquire for me in Baggot Street
And what I was like to know.
O he was a queer one,
Fol dol the di do,
He was a queer one
I tell you.

My great-grandmother knew him well,
He asked her to come and call
On him in his flat and she giggled at the thought
Of a young girl's lovely fall.
O he was dangerous,
Fol dol the di do,
He was dangerous
I tell you.

On Pembroke Road look out for my ghost,
Dishevelled with shoes untied,
Playing through the railings with little children
Whose children have long since died.
O he was a nice man,
Fol dol the di do,
He was a nice man
I tell you.

Go into a pub and listen well
If my voice still echoes there,
Ask the men what their grandsires thought
And tell them to answer fair.
O he was eccentric,
Fol dol the di do,
He was eccentric
I tell you.

He had the knack of making men feel
As small as they really were
Which meant as great as God had made them
But as males they disliked his air.
O he was a proud one,
Fol dol the di do,
He was a proud one
I tell you.

If ever you go to Dublin town
In a hundred years or so
Sniff for my personality,
Is it Vanity's vapour now?
O he was a vain one,
Fol dol the di do,
He was a vain one
I tell you.

I saw his name with a hundred others
In a book in the library,
It said he had never fully achieved
His potentiality.
O he was slothful,
Fol dol the di do,
He was slothful
I tell you.

He knew that posterity has no use
For anything but the soul,
The lines that speak the passionate heart,
The spirit that lives alone.
O he was a lone one,
Fol dol the di do
Yet he lived happily
I tell you.

NARCISSUS AND THE WOMEN

MANY women circled the prison of Reflection
Where he lay among the flashing mirrors
Hoping somewhere to find some door of Action
By which he might be rescued from his errors.

MEN are what they are, and what they do
Is their own business. If they praise
The gods or jeer at them, the gods can not
Be moved, involved or hurt. Serenely
The citizens of Parnassus look on
As Homer tells us, and never laugh
When any mortal has joined the party.

What happens in the small towns—
Hate, love, envy—is not
The concern of the gods. The poet poor,
Or pushed around, or to be hanged, retains
His full reality; and his authority
Is bogus if the sonorous beat is broken
By disturbances in human hearts—his own
Is detached, experimental, subject matter
For ironic analysis, even for pity
As for some stranger's private problem.

It is not cold on the mountain, human women
Fall like ripe fruit while mere men
Are climbing out on dangerous branches
Of banking, insurance and shops; going
To the theatre; becoming
Acquainted with actors; unhappily
Pretending to a knowledge of art.
Poet, you have reason to be sympathetic—
Count them the beautiful unbroken
And then forget them
As things aside from the main purpose
Which is to be
Passive, observing with a steady eye.

Now I must search till I have found my God—
Not in an orphanage. He hides
In no humanitarian disguise,
A derelict upon a barren bog;
But in some fantastically ordinary incog:
Behind a well-bred convent girl's eyes,
Or wrapped in middle-class felicities
Among the women in a coffee shop.
Surely my God is feminine, for Heaven
Is the generous impulse, is contented
With feeding praise to the good. And all
Of these that I have known have come from women.
While men the poet's tragic light resented,
The spirit that is Woman caressed his soul.

NINETEEN FIFTY-FOUR

NINETEEN fifty-four hold on till I try
To formulate some theory about you. A personal matter:
My lamp of contemplation you sought to shatter,
To leave me groping in madness under a low sky.
O I wish I could laugh! O I wish I could cry!
Or find some formula, some mystical patter
That would organize a perspective from this hellish
     scatter—
Everywhere I look a part of me is exiled from the I.
Therefore I must tell you before you depart my position;
Making the statement is enough—there are no answers
To any real question. But tonight I cannot sleep;
Two hours ago I heard the late homing dancers.
O Nineteen Fifty Four you leave and will not listen,
And do not care whether I curse or weep.

THERE was a time when a mood recaptured was enough
Just to be able to hold momentarily November in the
woods
Or a street we once made our own through being in
love.

But that is not enough now. The job is to answer
questions
Experience. Tell us what life has taught you. Not just
about persons—
Which is futile anyway in the long run—but a concrete,
as it were, essence.

The role is that of prophet and saviour. To smelt in
passion
The commonplaces of life. To take over the functions of
a god in a new fashion.
Ah! there is the question to speculate upon in lieu of an
answer.

HAVING CONFESSED

HAVING confessed he feels
That he should go down on his knees and pray
For forgiveness for his pride, for having
Dared to view his soul from the outside.
Lie at the heart of the emotion, time
Has its own work to do. We must not anticipate
Or awaken for a moment. God cannot catch us
Unless we stay in the unconscious room
Of our hearts. We must be nothing,
Nothing that God may make us something.
We must not touch the immortal material
We must not daydream to-morrow's judgement—
God must be allowed to surprise us.
We have sinned, sinned like Lucifer
By this anticipation. Let us lie down again
Deep in anonymous humility and God
May find us worthy material for His hand.

CANAL BANK WALK

LEAFY-WITH-LOVE banks and the green waters of the canal
Pouring redemption for me, that I do
The will of God, wallow in the habitual, the banal,
Grow with nature again as before I grew.
The bright stick trapped, the breeze adding a third
Party to the couple kissing on an old seat,
And a bird gathering materials for the nest for the Word
Eloquently new and abandoned to its delirious beat.
O unworn world enrapture me, enrapture me in a web
Of fabulous grass and eternal voices by a beech,
Feed the gaping need of my senses, give me ad lib
To pray unselfconsciously with overflowing speech
For this soul needs to be honoured with a new dress woven
From green and blue things and arguments that cannot be proven.

LINES WRITTEN ON A SEAT ON THE GRAND CANAL, DUBLIN, 'ERECTED TO THE MEMORY OF MRS DERMOT O'BRIEN'

O COMMEMORATE me where there is water,
Canal water preferably, so stilly
Greeny at the heart of summer. Brother
Commemorate me thus beautifully.
Where by a lock Niagariously roars
The falls for those who sit in the tremendous silence
Of mid-July. No one will speak in prose
Who finds his way to these Parnassian islands.
A swan goes by head low with many apologies,
Fantastic light looks through the eyes of bridges—
And look! a barge comes bringing from Athy
And other far-flung towns mythologies.
O commemorate me with no hero-courageous
Tomb—just a canal-bank seat for the passer-by.

DEAR FOLKS

JUST a line to remind my friends that after much trouble
Of one kind and another I am back in circulation.
I have recovered most of my heirlooms from the humps of rubble
That once was the house where I lived in the name of a nation.
And precious little I assure you was worth mind storage:
The images of half a dozen women who fell for the unusual,
For the Is that Is and the laughter-smothered courage,
The poet's. And I also found some crucial
Documents of sad evil that may yet
For all their ugliness and vacuous leers
Fuel the fires of comedy. The main thing is to continue,
To walk Parnassus right into the sunset
Detached in love where pygmies cannot pin you
To the ground like Gulliver. So good luck and cheers.

IT CAME as a pleasant surprise
To find experience
Where I feared that I
Had no such currency,
Had idled to a void
Without a wife or child,
I had been looking at
Field, gates, lakes, all that
Was part and parcel of
The wild breast of love.
In other fellows' wives
I lived a many lives
And here another cries:
My husband I despise
And truth is my true
Husband is you.

So I take my cloak of gold
And stride across the world
A knight of chivalry
Seeking some devilry
The winter trees rise up
And wave me on, a clap
Of falling rock declares
Enthusiasm; flares
Announce a reception committee
For me entering a city
And all this for an unthrifty
Man turned of fifty;

An undisciplined person
Through futile excitements arising
Finds in his spendthrift purse
A bankbook writ in verse
And borrowers of purity
Offering substantial security
To him who just strayed
Through a lifetime without a trade,
Him, him the ne'er-
Do-well a millionaire.

THE HOSPITAL *sonnet*

A YEAR ago I fell in love with the functional ward
Of a chest hospital: square cubicles in a row
Plain concrete, wash basins—an art lover's woe,
Not counting how the fellow in the next bed snored.
But nothing whatever is by love debarred,
The common and banal her heat can know.
The corridor led to a stairway and below
Was the inexhaustible adventure of a gravelled yard.

This is what love does to things: the Rialto Bridge,
The main gate that was bent by a heavy lorry,
The seat at the back of a shed that was a suntrap.
Naming these things is the love-act and its pledge;
For we must record love's mystery without claptrap,
Snatch out of time the passionate transitory.

*You can find beauty
in any common thing —*

153

IS

THE important thing is not
To imagine one ought
Have something to say,
A raison d'être, a plot for the play.
The only true teaching
Subsists in watching
Things moving or just colour
Without comment from the scholar.
To look on is enough
In the business of love.
Casually remark
On a deer running in a park;
Mention water again
Always virginal,
Always original,
It washes out Original Sin.
Name for the future
The everydays of nature
And without being analytic
Create a great epic.
Girls in red blouses,
Steps up to houses,
Sunlight round gables,
Gossip's young fables,
The life of a street.

O wealthy me! O happy state!
With an inexhaustible theme
I'll die in harness,
I'll die in harness with my scheme.

TO HELL WITH COMMONSENSE

MORE kicks than pence
We get from commonsense
Above its door is writ
All hope abandon. It
Is a bank will refuse a post
Dated cheque of the Holy Ghost.
Therefore I say to hell
With all reasonable
Poems in particular
We want no secular
Wisdom plodded together
By concerned fools. Gather
No moss you rolling stones
Nothing thought out atones
For no flight
In the light.
Let them wear out nerve and bone
Those who would have it that way
But in the end nothing that they
Have achieved will be in the shake up
In the final Wake Up
And I have a feeling
That through the hole in reason's ceiling
We can fly to knowledge
Without ever going to college.

FREEDOM

TAKE me to the top of the high hill
Mount Olympus laughter-roaring unsolemn
Where no one is angry and satirical
About a mortal creature on a tall column.

THEY took away the water-wheel,
Scrap-ironed all the corn-mill;
The water now cascades with no
Audience pacing to and fro
Taking in with casual glance
Experience.

The cold wet blustery winter day
And all that's happening will stay
Alive in the mind: the bleak
Water-flushed meadows speak
An enduring story
To a man indifferent in a doorway.

Packaged, pre-cooked flakes have left
A land of that old mill bereft.
The ghosts that were so local coloured
Hiding behind bags of pollard
Have gone from those empty walls.
The weir still curves its waterfalls
But lets them drop in the tailrace
No longer wildly chivalrous.

And with this mention we withdraw
To things above the temporal law.

LOVE IN A MEADOW

SHE waved her body in the circle sign
Of love purely born without side;
The earth's contour, she orbited to my pride,
Sin and unsin.
But the critic asking questions ran
From the fright of the dawn
To weep later on an urban lawn
For the undone
God-gifted man.
O the river flowed round and round
The low meadows filled with buttercups
In a place called Toprass.
I was born on high ground.

YELLOW VESTMENT

LATELY I have been travelling by a created guidance,
I invented a Superintendent, symbol henceforth vaster
Than Jupiter, Prometheus or a Chinese deity in alabaster.
For love's sake we must only consider whatever widens
The field of the faithful's activity. See over there
Water-lilies waiting to be enchanted by a folk song chanted.
On the road we walk nobody is unwanted;
With no hate in his heart or resentment each may wear
The arrogant air that goes with a yellow vestment.
Do not be worried about what the neighbours will say,
Deliver your judgment, you are independent
Of the man in the pub whose word is essential to happiness,
Who gives you existence. O sing to me some roundelay
And wear with grace the power-invoking habit.

No, no, no, I know I was not important as I moved
Through the colourful country, I was but a single
Item in the picture, the namer not the beloved.
O tedious man with whom no gods commingle.
Beauty, who has described beauty? Once upon a time
I had a myth that was a lie but it served:
Trees walking across the crests of hills and my rhyme
Cavorting on mile-high stilts and the unnerved
Crowds looking up with terror in their rational faces.
O dance with Kitty Stobling I outrageously
Cried out-of-sense to them, while their timorous paces
Stumbled behind Jove's page boy paging me.
I had a very pleasant journey, thank you sincerely
For giving me my madness back, or nearly.

MISS UNIVERSE

I LEARNED, I learned—when one might be inclined
To think, too late, you cannot recover your losses—
I learned something of the nature of God's mind,
Not the abstract Creator but He who caresses
The daily and nightly earth; He who refuses
To take failure for an answer till again and again is worn.
Love is waiting for you, waiting for the violence that she chooses
From the tepidity of the common round beyond exhaustion or scorn
What was once is still and there is no need for remorse;
There are no recriminations in Heaven. O the sensual throb
Of the explosive body, the tumultuous thighs!
Adown a summer lane comes Miss Universe
She whom no lecher's art can rob
Though she is not the virgin who was wise.

THE ONE

GREEN, blue, yellow and red—
God is down in the swamps and marshes
Sensational as April and almost incredible the flowering of our catharsis.
A humble scene in a backward place
Where no one important ever looked
The raving flowers looked up in the face
Of the One and the Endless, the Mind that has baulked
The profoundest of mortals. A primrose, a violet,
A violent wild iris—but mostly anonymous performers
Yet an important occasion as the Muse at her toilet
Prepared to inform the local farmers
That beautiful, beautiful, beautiful God
Was breathing His love by a cut-away bog.

OCTOBER

O LEAFY yellowness you create for me
A world that was and now is poised above time,
I do not need to puzzle out Eternity
As I walk this arboreal street on the edge of a town.
The breeze too, even the temperature
And pattern of movement is precisely the same
As broke my heart for youth passing. Now I am sure
Of something. Something will be mine wherever I am.
I want to throw myself on the public street without caring
For anything but the prayering that the earth offers.
It is October over all my life and the light is staring
As it caught me once in a plantation by the fox coverts.
A man is ploughing ground for winter wheat
And my nineteen years weigh heavily on my feet.

WINTER

CHRISTMAS, someone mentioned, is almost upon us
And looking out my window I saw that Winter had landed
Complete with the grey cloak and the bare tree sonnet
A scroll of bark hanging down to the knees as he scanned it
The gravel in the yard was pensive, annoyed to be crunched
As people with problems in their faces drive in in cars
Yet I with such solemnity around me refused to be bunched
In fact was inclined to give the go-by to bars.
Yes, there were things in that winter arrival that made me
Feel younger, less of a failure, it was actually earlier
Than many people thought; there were possibilities
For love, for South African adventure, for fathering a baby
For taking oneself in hand, catching on without a scare me, or
Taking part in a world war, joining up at the start of hostilities.

THE SELF-SLAVED

ME I will throw away.
Me sufficient for the day
The sticky self that clings
Adhesions on the wings
To love and adventure,
To go on the grand tour
A man must be free
From self-necessity.

See over there
A created splendour
Made by one individual
From things residual
With all the various
Qualities hilarious
Of what
Hitherto was not:

A November mood
As by one man understood;
Familiar, an old custom
Leaves falling, a white frosting
Bringing a sanguine dream
A new beginning with an old theme.

Throw away thy sloth
Self, carry off my wrath
With its self-righteous
Satirising blotches.
No self, no self-exposure
The weakness of the proser
But undefeatable
By means of the beatable.

I will have love, have love
From anything made of
And a life with a shapely form
With gaiety and charm
And capable of receiving
With grace the grace of living
And wild moments too
Self when freed from you.
Prometheus calls me on.
Prometheus calls me: Son,
We'll both go off together
In this delightful weather.

IN MEMORY OF MY MOTHER

I DO not think of you lying in the wet clay
Of a Monaghan graveyard; I see
You walking down a lane among the poplars
On your way to the station, or happily

Going to second Mass on a summer Sunday—
You meet me and you say:
'Don't forget to see about the cattle—'
Among your earthiest words the angels stray.

And I think of you walking along a headland
Of green oats in June,
So full of repose, so rich with life—
And I see us meeting at the end of a town

On a fair day by accident, after
The bargains are all made and we can walk
Together through the shops and stalls and markets
Free in the oriental streets of thought.

O you are not lying in the wet clay,
For it is a harvest evening now and we
Are piling up the ricks against the moonlight
And you smile up at us—eternally.

SURELY you would not ask me to have known
Only the passion of primrose banks in May
Which are merely a point of departure for the play
And yearning poignancy when on their own.
Yet when all is said and done a considerable
Portion of living is found in inanimate
Nature, and a man need not feel miserable
If fate should have decided on this plan of it.
Then there is always the passing gift of affection
Tossed from the windows of high charity
In the office girl and civil servant section
And these are no despisable commodity.
So be reposed and praise, praise praise
The way it happened and the way it is.

3

LECTURE HALL

To SPEAK in summer in a lecture hall
About literature and its use
I pick my brains and tease out all
To see if I can choose
Something untarnished, some new news

From experience that has been immediate,
Recent, something that makes
The listener or reader
Impregnant, something that reinstates
The poet. A few words like birth-dates

That brings him back in the public mind,
I mean the mind of the dozen or so
Who constantly listen out for the two-lined
Message that announces the gusto
Of the dead arisen into the sun-glow.

Someone in America will note
The apparent miracle. In a bar
In Greenwich Village some youthful poet
Will mention it, and a similar
In London or wherever they are

Those pickers-up of messages that produce
The idea that underneath the sun
Things can be new as July dews—
Out of the frowsy, the second-hand won . . .
Keep at it, keep at it while the heat is on

I say to myself as I consider
Virginal crevices in my brain
Where the never-exposed will soon be a mother.
I search for that which has no stain,
Something discovered vividly and sudden.

Opening

IT WAS the Warm Summer, that landmark
In a child's mind, an infinite day
Sunlight and burnt grass
Green grasshoppers on the railway slopes
The humming of the wild bees
The whole summer during the school holidays
Till the blackberries appeared.
Yes, a tremendous time that summer stands
Beyond the grey finities of normal weather.

The Main Body

It's not nearly as bad as you'd imagine
Living among small farmers in the north of Ireland
They are for the most part the ordinary frightened
Blind brightened, referred to sometimes socially
As the underprivileged.
They cannot perceive Irony or even Satire
They start up with insane faces if
You break the newspaper moral code.
'Language' they screech 'you effing so and so'
And you withdraw into a precarious silence
Organising in your mind quickly, for the situation is tense,
The theological tenets of the press.

There's little you can do about some
Who roar horribly as you enter a bar
Incantations of ugliness, words of half a syllable
Locked in malicious muteness full of glare.
And your dignity thinks of giving up the beer.

But I, trained in the slum pubs of Dublin
Among the most offensive class of all—
The artisans—am equal to this problem;
I let it ride and there is nothing over.

I understand through all these years
That my difference in their company is an intrusion
That tears at the sentimental clichés
They can see my heart squirm when their star rendites
The topmost twenty in the lowered lights.
No sir, I did not come unprepared.

Oddly enough I begin to think of Saint Poverty
Moving in this milieu (of his own time of course)
How did he work the oracle?
Was he an old fraud, a non-poet
Who is loved for his non-ness
Like any performer?

I protest here and now and forever
On behalf of all my peoples who believe in Verse
That my intention is not satire but humaneness
An eagerness to understand more about sad man
Frightened man, the workers of the world
Without being savaged in the process.
Broadness is my aim, a broad road where the many
Can see life easier—generally.

Here I come to a sticky patch
A personal matter that perhaps
Might be left as an unrevealed hinterland
For our own misfortunes are mostly unimportant.
But that wouldn't do.
So with as little embarrassment as possible I tell
How I was done out of a girl,
Not as before by a professional priest but by
The frightened artisan's morality.

It was this way.
She, a shopgirl of nineteen or less
Became infatuated by the old soldier,
The wide travelled, the sin-wise.
Desdemona-Othello idea.
O holy spirit of infatuation
God's gift to this poetic nation!

One day her boss caught her glance.
'You're looking in his eyes' he said.
From then on all the powers of the lower orders—
Perhaps all orders—were used to deprive me of my prize
Agamemnon's Briseis.
It soured me a bit as I had
Everything planned, no need to mention what,
Except that it was August evening under whitethorn
And early blackberries.

In many ways it is a good thing to be cast into exile
Among strangers
Who have no inkling
Of The Other Man concealed
Monstrously musing in a field.
For me they say a Rosary
With many a glossary.

NOTHING more to be done in that particular
Direction, nothing now but prayer—
Watching, regarding, piecing together a new curricula.
An un-angry enumerator
Handling all sorts of littleness as it has to be handled
As if it were in the eyes
Enormous as an English biographer's tittle-tattle
All held low so gossip can settle
Close in the nest
I brooding must itemise
Consider every colour and marking
Search out for letters
Pretend I am interested in important writers.
    That's not the game no more,
    We have no game no more
Must catch that rhyme that up there I left parking

    We have no game no more
    Some one stole our game
    And left us high and dry
    On a beliefless shore
    But it ain't no shame
Plainly the only thing is not to be a bore
To ourselves; no more to it than that
I have to live here in the country till I get a flat.

When first walking along these roads
Nobody but myself walked there
But wait a minute, an hour a day
There are men and women behaving
There are girls in troubled love
And all that I need to do is weave the action
And many may do things quite valuable.

Form.
Life At Work—Do not Disturb.
I am independent now.

I know what I must write if I can
This is the beginning of my Five Year Plan
Concerned am I with the activities of my own man.

And a week ago I idled,
That is to say I roared and cursed over the position
Broke, I had a good excuse for not caring
Arts Council croppers harvesting and sharing
And my deserted village all ill-faring
Activity on every front
And nought for the poor bastard who bore the brunt
Of the day's battle—blood and sweat and grunt
Satire a desert that yields no ——
As I have mentioned on many an occasion
Living in the country is a hard old station.

In the pubs everyone talks about age
My age, they know it to a day
No use lying on that score
I could get away from it all if I had a motor.

I must remember to absorb
Like a sponge, not disturb
By projecting my knowledge
It's hard work at Experience's college.

When drawn into involvement with the barmaid
By sharp-nosed fellows from the Assistant Mountains
Of Castleblaney
I will let the embarrassment run its course
Be rather glad
A little of this is good.
To be always protected by a bodyguard
Of reserve, remoteness—putting them in their place
With a word from There
Is quite unhard
But no use when you return to a vacant room.
Now that I've cottoned on to holy hoarding
Pelman himself could not increase my wording
To take it at its least value

I never suffer from malnu-
Trition. Or need for grog
I make a product I can easily flog
I am a small country exporting
The pill of meaning to those
Whom the condition is hurting
At this moment I can make spells
Whatever I say goes
Come London-Irish to me your voided souls
Shall not be left unfilled
I am more than a pub or club
I am the madhouse that spilled,
Spills, the true reason
The abandoned laughing of the free
You were Behaned in Egypt
And the alien-milled
Corn had no vitamins of hope
You're ill poor folks and suffering from gripe.

And all this is a mere side-product. Into me never entered
Care for you. I am self-centered
But bunch of bums
I throw you these bewitching crumbs
I give you the womb
Of the poem.

In the disused railway siding
(O railway that came up from Enniskillen)
A new living is spreading
Dandelions that grow from wagon-grease
I stand on the platform
And peace, perfect peace
Descends on me.

I said to Maggie a most purist maid
Can you explain the modern parade
Of tycoons sultaning it with shabby whores
Notorious nobodys in a world of bores
She said that that was twentieth-century play
As we lay together on an ex-railway

She said all public heroes were the same
From pimp descended and the poxy dame
Glittering in dinner dress in brass tiaras
No poet could be interested in those arses
I saw that this was probably the case
Private beauty and green happiness
Demand much courage. And I recalled
Being asked by poor fellows if I willed
Their right to enjoy a picture say or book
So glad when I gave the green light were those folk
They had enjoyed that most uproarious play
And were so glad that they had laughed.

Away

Begone dull care thou has not got a chance
The rapturous eagles soar us up from Hence
To Thence
From Sense.

My love lies at the gates of foam
The last dear wreck of day
And William H. Burroughs collages the poem
As the curfew tolls the knell of Gray.

No SYSTEM, no Plan,
Yeatsian invention
No all-over
Organisational prover.
Let words laugh
And people be stimulated by our stuff.

Michelangelo's Moses
Is one of the poses
Of Hemingway
Jungle-crashing after prey
Beckett's garbage-can
Contains all our man
Who without fright on his face
Dominates the place
And makes all feel
That all is well.

Yet without smuggery
Of the smirk of buggery
Or any other aid
We have produced our god
And everyone present
Become godded and pleasant
Confident, gay—
No remorse that a day
Can show no output
Except from the gut.

In the Name of The Father
The Son and The Mother
We explode
Ridiculously, uncode
A habit and find therein
A successful human being.

ANOTHER summer, another July
People going on holiday, women in light dresses
How I once jealously feared for them under the
    printed cotton
Limp unresisting to any man's caresses.

I would have one of my own
And then like other men I could make cynical
    remarks
At the dangers they ran and never be worried about
    summer
And what happens in the shelter of parks.

As it is I praise the rain
For washing out the bank holiday with its moral risks
It is not a nice attitude but it is conditioned by
    circumstances
And by a childhood perverted by Christian moralists.

THE GAMBLER: A BALLET WITH WORDS

EXPLANATION

HERE we have a work of fiction, purporting
To portray the ways of the poet-artist,
It has gone wrong in places, missed
The secret of love—the gift
Of the poet's knowledge that is subject to no sporting
Chance on a wheel. The idealist
Is a man sick for art's panacea, courting
Remote beauties. But the poet's snorting
Is for schoolgirls or large women full of drive.
Roulette life is for fools. Being alive—
Surprisingly quite rare—is a solid factor,
But we must conventionalise for the actor
And play the artifices to show the true.

For the artifice cold and implacable
Has an inhuman beauty for our pleasure
The dancers are a veritable treasure
In a world so noisily cacable.
From a normal viewpoint they are untackable
Stylised sex sinful but inbackable
Essentially as toys meant
Unlike Annie Besant
Whose backside was quite whackable
When we want to be withdrawn they are the answer
To many problems in a television society.
You are in a low pub reading the paper
And you see in the monstrous mirrors the sleething dancer
Who demands of you no emotional moiety
Or your attention as he capes his caper.

HERE we go round the mystic wheel
Dancing a wild Gaelic reel
Gambling on the ideal.

I have nothing to announce
On any subject yet one
I was full of bounce

At what I can't say
At this time of day
But it was all felt violently

By god and by guss
It's not that but this
Like Wyndham Lewis.

The theme here invented
And by me pa-tented
Psychology bended

Is about a poor hero
Who gambled on Zero
There's no rhyme but Nero.

Happiness can be achieved
This hero believed
As the roulette wheel revved.

And so it can
Happen to a man
That's the tan—

Talising thing
We nearly made it sing
Great glory to the king.

This sad fool
Knew he could scoop the pool
Of the beautiful

Have a beauty of vast sexuality
And brutality
Not the ideal but the actuality.

Such is our act
Not quite divorced from fact
By fate we are racked.

He danced with the red
Even money to bed
But no maidenhead

He danced with the black
Who will fall on her back
For a twopenny smack

While he plays his high jinks
It's much later than he thinks
He'll be alone with his drinks.

There's only eighty years at most
And he cannot see his own interest
Tawdry marriage at best.

Zero is just
A thin aspect of lust
O huge thighs, enormous bust

And see the schoolgirls
Repugnant to morals
Wait by the pillars

The key of all treasure
The secret of pleasure
Is what you can measure.

He plays for disaster
Some slow and some faster
I am Fate and the master

I am Art and not life
I will give him a wife
And a houseful of strife.

She roars in my rhyme
I want him him
To rip me in twain.

Unmaiden me with ferocity
There's nothing like audacity
For a virgin's capacity
On no ceremony stand
You've the whip in your hand
I'm at your command.

The croupier Fate
Is in quite a state
When I tell him to quit.

I the king
Decide everything
Dancers you've had your fling.

I choose
A sixteen year old muse
For my idealist. Here's news
Disperse, die fade
Fool, unmaid
Zero
Hero
You've the tools of the trade

There's really nothing one can say
Useful we all mess up our play
And fail any old way.

NEWS ITEM

In Islington for the moment I reside
A hen's race from Cheapside
Where Tom the peeping sun first eyed.

Where Gilpin's horse had bolted
All the traffic halted
The man on board was malted.

And in these romantic lots
I run into Paul Potts
Noticing the pull of roots.

I have taken roots of love
And will find it pain to move.
Betjeman, you've missed much of

The secrets of London while
Old churches you beguile
I'll show you a holier aisle—

The length of Gibson Square
Caught in November's stare
That would set you to prayer.

Dickens—all the clichés
Revert to the living species
Ideas with the impact of Nietzsche's.

I walk in Islington Green
Finest landscape you ever seen
I'm as happy as I've ever been.

THE sun is hot, long days, yet summer
Finds me very little dumber
Than last winter in grey old London

Lying on a bed in a basement, unable
To lift my sickness to a fable,
Hating the sight of a breakfast table.

On Christmas Day stretched out, how awful
Not heeding the Church's orders lawful
While everyone else is having a crawful.

It is black all round as terror stricken
I climb stone steps, trying not to weaken,
My legs are taking a terrible licking.

To the King Edward, empty of pudds
Two friends and I in crumpled duds
Go to talk with John Heath-Stubbs.

O Charles Dickens with your Scrooge
I would gladly have taken refuge,
I was as sick as the devil's puke.

I try to be merry those three lit hours
Then back to the subterranean fires
Drinking whisky to the sound of lyres.

Odd how such things six months later
Leap up as laughter's instigator
From the depths of that Paddington crater.

I must avoid being unfrank
The plain truth is that I drank
More than would kill a New York yank.

And verse that can redeem a soul
And make a body beautiful
I did not work at it at all.

O there is a Muse not good and gracious
But long suffering, and tenacious
She will not have a man stay stocious.

I hope I am not being clammy,
The whisky bottle I loved like mammy
The curse of drink! let's not get hammy.

I just want to assure all
That a poem made is a cure-all
Of any soul-sickness. Toolooral!

Today in the street I was astonished
The years had left me so unpunished,
I was in love with women—honest!

The Word is the messenger of the eye.
The old canal is as full of blue sky
As a year ago and so kind to I.

That Grand Canal into which I was pushed
At wetting me must have surely blushed.
The men who did the job were cursed:

I had praised it in many a sonnet
And the dear swans that lived upon it—
So for the grudgers to hell or Connaught!

Now I must speak to people but keep intact
The virginal knowledge, converse about fact
Newspaper news of some international pact.

It is only twelve o'clock noon
And I have experienced about one
Millionth of a day begun.

I meet a man whom I once had pumped
With ideas, he was sad and humped
Like a market that had downward slumped.

The ideas I had upon him forced
Were gone and left him much worse the worst
And to think how amusingly he had discoursed.

Very nearly a poet complete with irony,
Knowledged in every literary joinery,
He used to dress in poetic finery.

And then he leaked and although I strove
To fill him with the breath of love
The fatal puncture still blew off.

It was sad to see the empty bag
Blown about like a dirty rag.
But let us be humble and never brag.

The way things were going he thought my stuff
Contained far too much Parnassian guff,
As a businessman he had had enough.

So I went on my way carrying the flame
On to the ultimate Olympic Game
Where no one belonging ever gives in.

Out of weakness more than muscle
Relentlessly men continue to tussle
With the human-eternal puzzle.

There were gulls on the pond in St Stephen's Park
And many things worth a remark.
I sat on a deck-chair and started to work

On a morning's walk not quite effectual,
A little too unselectual
But what does it count in the great perpetual?

I revert once more to those limpid arses
Which for me can give the ideal catharsis,
But the memory of what's lost saddens and embarrasses.

I must be content with the roses—
But sitting in deck-chairs Holy Moses!
University girls here in roly-poses.

I certainly enjoyed myself thoroughly
Rambling idly and rather amorally
For a whole hour. Now surely

I can lie on the grass, feel no remorse
For idling, I have worked at verse
And exorcised a winter's curse.

A BALLAD

O CRUEL are the women of Dublin's fair city
They smile out of cars and are gone in a flash,
You know they are charming and gay in their
    hearts
And would laugh as vivaciously buried in chaff
As they would underneath a pink shower of
    confetti.

I knew one in Baggot Street, a medical student
Unless I am greatly mistaken is she;
Her smile plays a tune on my trembling psyche
At thirty yards range, but she passes by me
In a frost that would make Casanova be prudent.

It's the same everywhere—the wish without
    will,
And it tortures, yet I would not change it for
    all
The women from Bond Street right down to
    The Mall,
For wealth is potential, not the remedies at call,
I say as I walk down from Baggot Street Bridge.

HE was an egoist with an unsocial conscience,
And I liked him for it though he was out of favour,
For he seemed to me to be sincere,
Wanting to be no one but his own saviour.

He saw the wild eyes that are the Public's
Turned on the one man who held
Against the gangs of fear his ordinary soul—
He did no public service but lived for himself.

His one enthusiasm was against the hysteria,
Those dangerous men who are always in procession
Searching for someone to murder or worship—
He never qualified for directorship or a State
    pension.

AN INSULT

I CAME to a great house on the edge of a park
Thinking on Yeats' dream Great House where all
Nobility was protected by ritual
Though all lay drunk on the floor and in the dark
Tough louts and menial minds in the shrubberies lurk
And negative eunuchs hate in an outer hall.
The poet and lover is sage though from grace
    he fall
Temporarily. The Evil Barbarian dare not work
The servile spell, the insult of a fool
To which there is no answer but to pray
For guidance through the parks of every day
To be silent till the soul itself forgives,
To learn again there is no golden rule
For keeping out of suffering—if one lives.

ON RAGLAN ROAD

(Air: *The Dawning of The Day*)

ON Raglan Road on an autumn day I met her first and knew
That her dark hair would weave a snare that I might
    one day rue;
I saw the danger, yet I walked along the enchanted way,
And I said, let grief be a fallen leaf at the dawning of
    the day.

On Grafton Street in November we tripped lightly along
    the ledge
Of the deep ravine where can be seen the worth of
    passion's pledge,
The Queen of Hearts still making tarts and I not making
    hay—
O I loved too much and by such by such is happiness
    thrown away.

I gave her gifts of the mind I gave her the secret sign
    that's known
To the artists who have known the true gods of sound
    and stone
And word and tint. I did not stint for I gave her poems
    to say.
With her own name there and her own dark hair like
    clouds over fields of May.

On a quiet street where old ghosts meet I see her
    walking now
Away from me so hurriedly my reason must allow
That I had wooed not as I should a creature made of
    clay—
When the angel wooes the clay he'd lose his wings at
    the dawn of day.

I AM here in a garage in Monaghan.
It is June and the weather is warm,
Just a little bit cloudy. There's the sun again
Lifting to importance my sixteen acre farm.
There are three swallows' nests in the rafters above me
And the first clutches are already flying.
Spread this news, tell all if you love me,
You who knew that when sick I was never dying
(Nae gane, nae gane, nae frae us torn
But taking a rest like John Jordan).
                                    Other exclusive
News stories that cannot be ignored:
I climbed Woods' Hill and the elusive
Underworld of the grasses could be heard,
John Lennon shouted across the valley,
Then I saw a new June moon, quite as stunning
As when young we blessed the sight as something holy . . .
Sensational adventure that is only beginning.

For I am taking this evening walk through places
High up among the Six Great Wonders,
The power privileges, the unborn amazes
The unplundered
Where man with no meaning blooms
Large in the eyes of his females:
He doesn't project, nor even assumes
The loss of one necessary believer.
It's as simple as that, it's a matter
Of walking with the little gods, the ignored
Who are so seldom asked to write the letter
Containing the word
O only free gift! no need for Art any more
When Authority whispers like Tyranny at the end of a bar.

SENSATIONAL DISCLOSURES!

(KAVANAGH TELLS ALL)

KAVANAGH tells all,
Lays bare his soul
For the good of his neighbours
And the Sunday papers.
Patiently he labours
To advise and warn
Poets soft in the horn.
Rising from his own dirt
He sends this sensational report:

He frittered away
A talent that could flay
D. J. Enright—say;
He could disburse
A fabulosity of verse,
Could swallow without dodgery
Ted Hughes' menagerie,
He often spat forth
Lions of more wrath.

But Kavanagh, the dog,
Took to the grog
Leaving Larkin and Logue
Manufacturing fog,
And even MacNeice
Making ground in the race.

But he'll have the last laugh
On Davie and Hough
For as he went wandering
In a valley, deep thundering
From long-muted fellows
Conspired in some hello's
To halt him as he rambled,
Drank brandy and gambled:

O Kavanagh repent
And start to invent
An amenable myth
Of everyday width
To meet every condition
Outside genuine passion.
Learn to shovel:
A bulldozer novel.
Make critical works
Like those industrious jerks
Who don't even relax
When they go to the jakes.

Gladden our days
With musical plays—
And profoundest believer
Write prayers for the Beaver.
And then of the sum
Make a megaton bomb.

So he sailed up the Cydnus
To Chatto and Windus
And with one cannonade
Wrecked the critical trade.

Rumble and roar
In the poetry war.
American bums
Change the angle of thumbs
And get on the blower
To find out the score
(Post Spanish Civil War.)
Oscar Williams is sore
Screaming to harass
The heart of Alvarez,
Starts to eat till he'll founder
The files of *Encounter*.
'Why wasn't I told
Of new gallups polled?'

The battle is on,
There are gasps from Thom Gunn
Elizabeth Jennings
Suspends all her pennings,
To meet new assessments
Edith burns her vestments.

And that's how it was
When Kavanagh uprose
From his dosshouse of filth
In vulgar good health.
Next week he'll reveal
All about the smell
From Soviet poets who rebel
Against what is dead,
Reminiscent of Hampstead.

Tame, tame, tame, tame,
Kavanagh lifts the lid of same
Exposes all the guilty men,
The selectors of the team.

THE SAME AGAIN

I HAVE my friends, my public and they are waiting
For me to come again as their one and only bard
With a new statement that will repay all the waitment
While I was hitting the bottle hard.
I know it is not right to be light and flippant
There are people in the streets who steer by my star.
There was nothing they could do but view me while I threw
Back large whiskeys in the corner of a smoky bar
And if only I would get drunk it wouldn't be so bad
With a pain in my stomach I wasn't even comic
Swallowing every digestive pill to be had.
Some of my friends stayed faithful but quite a handful
Looked upon it as the end: I could quite safely be
Dismissed a dead loss in the final up toss.
He's finished and that's definitely.

THANK YOU, THANK YOU

... PARTICULARLY if yourself
Have been left as they call it on the shelf
All God's chillun got wings
So the black Alabaman sings.

Down Grafton Street on Saturdays
Don't grieve like Marcus Aurelius
Who said that though he grew old and grey
The people of the Appian Way
Were always the same pleasant age
Twenty-four on average.

I can never help reflecting
Of coming back in another century
From now and feeling comfortable
At a buzzing coffee table,
The students in 2056
With all the old eternal tricks.

The thing that I most glory in
Is this exciting unvarying
Quality that withal
Is completely original.

For what it teaches is just this
We are not alone in our loneliness,
Others have been here and known
Griefs we thought our special own
Problems that we could not solve
Lovers that we could not have
Pleasures that we missed by inches.
Come I'm beginning to get pretentious
Beginning to message for instead
Of expressing how glad
I am to have lived to feel the radiance
Of a holy hearing audience
And delivered God's commands

Into those caressing hands,
My personality that's to say
All that is mine exclusively.
What wisdom's ours if such there be
Is a flavour of personality.
I thank you and I say how proud
That I have been by fate allowed
To stand here having the joyful chance
To claim my inheritance
For most have died the day before
The opening of that holy door.

Epilogue to a series of lectures given at University College, Dublin

THE day I walked out on Reason—that old plodder
(But you didn't)
Was the best day of my life; it would take years
To tell of the dirty he did on me, the love-fodder
That other bulls backchewed for me in several gears.
(Catholic peasant)
It is too embarrassing to talk about love misses
And pleases those we ought not entertain.
She gave herself! Oh no! There were only kisses
The listener cannot endure the possible gain.
To tell the tale is needless repetition
But they did come with all heroic violence
(For that I'll vouch
On any couch)
But Reason always intruded on the session
Or perhaps it was the conscience of cold climates.
(Unwilling saint,
A moot point)
Well, call it what you like.

THAT GARAGE

THE lilacs by the gate
The summer sun again
The swallows in and out
Of the garage where I am.
The sound of land activity
Machinery in gear
This is not longevity
But infinity.
Perhaps a little bit
Too facilely romantic
We must stop and struggle with
A mood that's getting frantic
Getting Georgian
Richard Church and Binyon
O stand and plan
More difficult dominion.

I

I AM here all morning with the familiar
Blank page in front of me, I have perused
An American anthology for stimulation
But the result is not encouraging as it used
To be when Walter Lowenfel's falling down words
Like ladders excited me to chance my arm
With nouns and verbs.   ⌐ gorse
But the wren, the wren got caught in the furze
And the eagle turned turkey on my farm.

II

Last summer I made a world fresh and fair,
(As the daughters of Erin) completely equipped
With everything for the full life. A wealth of experience
Of every kind waiting to be tapped.
I had a story, a career
Shaped like a statesman's for the biographer.
I had done all things in my time
And had not yet reached my prime.

III

Nature is not enough, I've used up lanes
Waters that run in rivers or are stagnant;
But I have no message and the sins
Of no red idea can make me pregnant.
So I sit tight to manufacture
A world word by word–machine–to–live–in structure—
That may in any garden be assembled
Where critics looking through the glass can lecture
On poets—X, Y and Z therein entempled.

INDEX OF FIRST LINES

INDEX OF FIRST LINES

A. R. Ammons *Briefings*
 Collected Poems: 1951–1971
 Tape for the Turn of the Year (Norton Library)
William Burford *A Beginning*
Jim Harrison *Locations*
 Plain Song
Richard Hugo *The Lady in Kicking Horse Reservoir*
Ronald Johnson *The Book of the Green Man*
 Valley of the Many-Colored Grasses
Milton Kaplan *In a Time Between Wars*
Patrick Kavanagh *Collected Poems* (Norton Library)
Robert Morgan *Red Owl*
Robert L. Peters *Songs for a Son*
Adrienne Rich *Diving into the Wreck: Poems 1971–1972*
 Leaflets: Poems 1965–1968
 Necessities of Life
 Snapshots of a Daughter-in-Law
 The Will to Change: Poems 1968–1970
Laura Riding *Selected Poems: In Five Sets*
May Sarton *Cloud, Stone, Sun, Vine*
 A Durable Fire
 A Grain of Mustard Seed
 A Private Mythology
Jean Starr Untermeyer *Job's Daughter*
Louis Zukofsky *All: The Collected Short Poems* (Norton Library)
 All: The Collected Short Poems, 1923–1958
 All: The Collected Short Poems, 1956–1964